Samsung S20 FE 5G Complete Guide

The Complete Illustrated, Practical Guide with Tips & Tricks to Maximizing your S20 FE like a Pro

Steve Woods

Copyright © 2020 by Steve Woods - All rights reserved.

All other copyrights & trademarks are the properties of their respective owners; Reproduction of any part of this book without the permission of the copyright owners is illegal-except with the inclusion of brief quotes in a review of the work.

Contents

Introduction 1

Chapter 1 10

Getting started: 10

    Device layout 10

    Set up your device 10

    Charge the battery 12

Chapter Two 15

Start using your device: 15

    Turn on your Device 15

    Use the Setup Wizard 15

    Transfer Data 16

    Lock or Unlock your Device 17

    Side key settings 17

    Accounts 18

    Set up voicemail 20

    Navigation 20

    Customize your home screen 28

    Easy mode 35

    Samsung Daily 40

    Bixby 41

    Digital wellbeing and parental controls 43

    Always On Display 44

    Biometric security 46

    Edge screen 55

Enter text 65

Emergency mode 69

Chapter 3 .... **73**

Camera and Gallery: **73**

Navigate the camera screen 74

Configure shooting mode 75

AR Zone 77

Live focus 78

Scene optimizer 78

Record videos 78

Live focus video 79

Super Slow-mo 79

Super steady 80

Camera settings 80

View pictures 85

Edit pictures 86

Play video 87

Video enhancer 88

Edit video 88

Share pictures and videos 89

Delete pictures and videos 89

Create movie 90

Take a screenshot 91

Screen recorder 91

Chapter 4 .... **94**

Using Apps: 94

Download apps 94

Uninstall or disable apps 94

Search for apps 94

Sort apps 95

Create and use folders 95

Game Booster 96

App settings 97

Galaxy Essentials 99

Samsung Health 140

Chapter 5 153
Settings: 153

Search for Settings 154

Wi-Fi 154

Bluetooth 158

NFC and payment 161

Airplane mode 162

Mobile networks 163

Data usage 164

Mobile hotspot 166

Tethering 169

Nearby device scanning 170

Connect to a printer 170

MirrorLink 171

Virtual Private Networks 171

Private DNS 173

Ethernet 173

Chapter 6 175
Customization, Security, Accounts & Backup: 175

Sounds and vibration 175

Sound mode 175

Vibrations 176

Volume 177

Ringtone 178

Notification sound 178

System sound 179

System sounds and vibration 179

Dolby Atmos 180

Equalizer 181

Headset audio options 181

Adapt sound 181

Separate app sound 182

Manage notifications 183

Customize app notifications 184

Smart alert 184

Smart pop-up view 185

Dark mode 185

Screen brightness 186

Blue light filter 187

Screen mode 187

Font size and style 188

Screen zoom 188

Full screen apps 189

Screen timeout 189

Accidental touch protection 189

Touch sensitivity 190

Show charging information 190

Screen saver 190

Reduce animations 191

Lift to wake 191

Double tap to wake 192

Smart stay 192

One-handed mode 192

Quick optimization 193

Battery 194

Storage 195

Memory 195

Advanced options 196

Language and input 197

Date and time 202

Troubleshooting 203

Screen lock types 209

Google Play Protect 212

Find My Mobile 212

Samsung Pass 213

Samsung Blockchain Keystore 214

Install unknown apps 214

Secure Folder 215

Secure Wi-Fi 215

View passwords 215

Device administration 216

Credential storage 216

Advanced security settings 217

Location 218

Permission manager 220

Send diagnostic data 221

Samsung Cloud 221

Add an account 222

Account settings 223

Remove an account 223

Backup and restore 223

Google settings 225

Chapter 7 226

Accessibility: 226

Screen Reader 226

Visibility enhancements 226

Hearing enhancements 229

Interaction and dexterity 231

Advanced settings 234

Installed services 236

About Accessibility 236

Tips and help 237

Dual Messenger 238

About phone 238

Chapter 8 240
Tips & Tricks 240

Hide Apps 240

Hide Front Cameras 241

In-Display Ultrasonic Fingerprint Scanner 242

Assistant Menu 243

Reverse Wireless Charging 244

Battery Percentage In Status Bar 245

One-Handed Mode 246

Hide Albums In Gallery 246

Dual Messenger 247

Use Edge Screen 248

Swipe Palm To Take Screenshot 249

Take Photos With Palm 250

Navigation Gestures 252

Double Tap To Wake Up 252

Enable Flashlight Notifications 253

Power & Volume Keys Shortcut 254

Enable Dark Mode(Night Mode) 255

Send Schedule Message 256

Lockdown Mode 257

Pin Windows Feature 259

The Auto Restart Feature 260

Lock Home Screen Layout 261

Lift to wake feature 261

Navigation Gestures 262

Samsung Galaxy S20, S20+, and S20 Ultra: Camera features and Tips 263

Index 266

Introduction

For those keeping score, Samsung released yet another phone — its 15th this year. The Galaxy S20 Fan Edition is a Frankenstein device, for which Samsung pulled what it deemed the "best" and "most important features" from the rest of the S20 family to build one monster of a device. And, at $699.99, it's an affordable hodgepodge of a smartphone.

Budget and performance harmonize beautifully with the Galaxy S20 FE. After using it for 11 days, we've found that Android performs in the ways we'd expect. The camera is dependable. A flat screen is super nice and means no more accidental touches. And the design, while not super high-end, doesn't feel like a cheap build.

It feels really good in the hand

Rather than a metal and glass build all around, Samsung swapped the glass back for a polycarbonate (read: plastic) back. It has a smooth matte finish that, at least with the Cloud Navy shade we tested, hides fingerprints pretty well (even when they were greasy after our all-important potato chip test). Dust and particles, though, do linger on top.

It's not glossy like glass, so it's easier to get a grip on. The point being, it still feels nice. It's well-made plastic, which is then surrounded by a metal frame that adds rigidity to the S20 FE. The 6.5-inch 1080p HD display on the front features a layer of Corning Gorilla Glass 5 to protect from scratches and dreaded drops. It's also a flat display, meaning the left and right sides don't curve down the sides toward the back. Other S20s feature this, along with the Moto Edge (you could say it capitalizes on that), but it doesn't provide much in terms of use cases. But the flat design here does eliminate accidental touches.

And let's get a bit more specific on the 6.5-inch screen: It's an FHD+ Super AMOLED Infinity-O display with a 1080 x 2400 resolution and 407 pixels per inch.

Most important for video playback and gaming would be the 120 Hz refresh rate. This measurement describes how many times in a second the screen refreshes itself. The higher the number, the better, and 120 Hz is the standard we wish every phone would reach. Whether you're watching a YouTube video or a feature film on the S20 FE, you're getting a TV-level experience. We also didn't experience any pixelation when zooming in on text. For most people, a 1080p display is just fine. It does feel a bit less vibrant than the S20 Ultra or Note 20 Ultra, though.

Toward the bottom of the display, in the center, is a fingerprint sensor. It's the same ultrasonic sensor found on other Samsung devices, and it performs well here. The more you use it, the easier it is to get the hang of it. It's a nice higher-end feature to have on this midrange device.

Rounding out the design is a volume rocker and power button on the right-hand side, a USB-C port and speaker on the bottom and a microSD card and SIM card slot on the top. The rear side does feature a slim camera bump with three cameras and an LED flash.

The S20 FE trucks along

The Galaxy S20 FE is powered by the same Qualcomm processor as the rest of the S20 family. The big difference is the amount of RAM, as the S20 FE features a modest 6GB of RAM compared to the rest of the S20s that feature up to 12GB. It's still ample enough to provide a runway for intense apps, multitasking and everyday use cases.

It might seem like a big number drop, but we didn't notice much performance difference when completing core tasks. Browsing social networks like TikTok, Instagram and Twitter was seamless. Productivity apps like Outlook, Gmail, Google Drive, Docs, Trello, Slack and a few others worked just fine, even with multiple applications open in the background.

Real Racing 3, Call of Duty: Mobile and streaming titles from Xbox Game Pass (via the xCloud streaming service) all performed well. The first two run on-device, while the latter is streamed in via the internet. We didn't notice any hangups with either approach, and the 120 Hz screen delivered a smooth experience.

Performance is really not a concern here, and it scored similarly to the rest of the S20 family in our tests. As with every CNN Underscored review, we ran the Galaxy S20 FE through a series of benchmarks to determine quantitative performance. In GeekBench 5 it scored a 900 on single-core and 3,197 on multi-core. In comparison, the Galaxy

S20 scored a 911 on a single-core and a 3,233 on multi-core, while the S20+ scored a 918 on single-core and a 3,274 on multi-core. So, yes, the quantitative matches up with the qualitative here.

Inside the Galaxy S20 FE is a large 4,500mAh battery. That's bigger than the battery in the A71 5G or Galaxy S20 from Samsung. We had no issues getting through a full day with 10 to 12 hours of use. It does support fast charging via a 25-watt brick, but Samsung only includes a 15-watt in the box. You can also charge it wirelessly or charge another device on the back with Wireless PowerShare.

And a quick note on 5G. As we always say, don't buy a device just for the 5G connectivity — networks are still young in the United States. If anything, buy a device that has appeal, and if it has 5G support, you're future-proofing yourself. The $699.99 Galaxy S20 FE only supports the sub6 connectivity, which is more prominent but a bit slower. There's a $749.99 Galaxy S20 FE that supports sub6 and mmWave, but it's exclusive to Verizon in the US.

Four cameras make for a solid shooting experience

In total there are four cameras on this $699.99 smartphone:

- **A 32-megapixel front-facing lens:** Perfect for selfies and video calls.
- **A 12-megapixel ultrawide lens:** Similar to other Samsung devices, this lens is great for capturing a wider frame of view with a focus on details.
- **A 12-megapixel wide-angle lens:** This is the default lens on the S20 FE and is also similar to other Samsung devices.

- **An 8-megapixel telephoto lens:** This was the big question, as it's the lowest-megapixel lens on any Samsung device that is powering Space Zoom (Samsung tech combining optical and digital zoom for getting extreme shots). The Galaxy S20 FE supports up to 30x Space Zoom.

You can see a full gallery of images shot on the Galaxy S20 FE below, along with a video test. On the latter, the Galaxy S20 FE supports up to 4K video recording. There's no 8K here like on the Note 20 Ultra, but most users won't really miss that.

Similarly, we were impressed with the 50x and 100x Space Zoom on the Note 20 Ultra and S20 Ultra. The Note 20 Ultra's addition of laser autofocus made it usable, but even at 50x it seems more like a party trick, as images still contain some blurs and quality losses. We found the 30x function to be the most reliable, along with 10x optical zoom.

So how does the 30x Space Zoom perform on the S20 FE? Well, it performs pretty admirably. Most 30x shots we captured indoors, zooming into a small object — like a

Lego figure — resulted in a loss of quality. This can depend on lighting, but it's clear that the sensor here performs a little less than what we would have hoped for. You're much better off sticking with the 10x zoom function or the 3x optical zoom.

Don't get us wrong, though — the S20 FE still captures some nice shots and gives you the advantages that come with three lenses in your pocket. Just take a look at our test photos below. There's some weirdness with how Samsung handles colors, saturation and white balance, though. Images often skew to warmer colors and up the saturation to high levels.

Chapter 1

Getting started

Device layout:

Samsung Galaxy S20 FE 5G

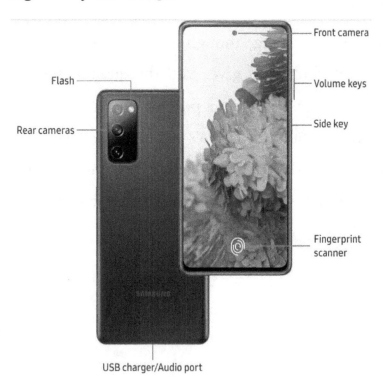

Set up your device

Your device uses a nano-SIM card. A SIM card may be preinstalled, or you may be able to use your previous SIM card. Network indicators for 5G service are based on your carrier's specifications and network availability.

NOTE - Use only charging devices and batteries (if applicable) that are approved by Samsung. Samsung charging devices and batteries are designed for your device to maximize battery life. Using other charging devices and batteries may void your warranty and may cause damage.

NOTE - Your device is IP68 rated for dust and water resistance. To maintain the water-resistant and dust-resistant features of your device, make sure that the SIM card/Memory card tray openings are maintained free of dust and water, and the tray is securely inserted prior to any exposure to liquids.

Charge the battery

Your device is powered by a rechargeable battery. A charger (charging head and USB Type-C cable) is included with the device for charging the battery from a power outlet.

TIP While charging, the device and the charger may become hot and stop charging. This usually does not affect the device's lifespan or performance and is in the device's normal range of operation. Disconnect the charger from the device and wait for the device to cool down.

Wireless PowerShare

Wirelessly charge your compatible Samsung devices using your phone. Some features are not available while sharing power.

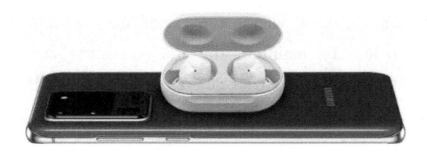

From Quick Settings, tap 🔘 Wireless PowerShare to enable this feature. With the phone face down, place the compatible device on the back of the phone to charge. A notification sound or vibration occurs when charging begins.

NOTE - Wireless PowerShare works with most Qi-Certified devices. Requires minimum 30% battery to share. Speed and power efficiency of charge varies by device. May not work with some accessories, covers, or other manufacturer's devices. If you have trouble connecting or charging is slow, remove any cover from each device. May affect call reception or data services, depending on your network environment.

For best results when using Wireless PowerShare:

- Remove any accessories or cover before using the feature. Depending on the type of accessory or cover, Wireless PowerShare may not work properly.
- The location of the wireless charging coil may vary by device, so you may need to adjust the placement

to make a connection. When charging starts, a notification or vibration will occur, so the notification will help you know you've made a connection.

- Call reception or data services may be affected, depending on your network environment.

- Charging speed or efficiency can vary depending on device condition or surrounding environment.

- Do not use headphones.

Chapter Two
Start using your device

Turn on your Device

Use the Side key to turn your device on. Do not use the device if the body is cracked or broken. Use the device only after it has been repaired.

- o Press and hold the Side key to turn the device on.

- To turn the device off, open the Notification panel and tap **Power** > **Power off**

- Confirm when prompted. To restart your device, open the Notification panel and tap **Power** > **Restart**. Confirm when prompted. **Tip:** You can also turn your device off by pressing the Side and Volume down keys at the same time. To learn more about powering off your device from Settings, tap **Advanced features** > **Side key** > **How to power off your phone**.

Use the Setup Wizard

The first time you turn your device on, the Setup Wizard guides you through the basics of setting up your device. Follow the prompts to choose a default language, connect to a Wi-Fi® network, set up accounts, choose location services, learn about your device's features, and more.

Transfer Data

Use Smart Switch™ to transfer contacts, photos, music, videos, messages, notes, calendars, and more from your old device. Smart Switch can transfer your data via USB cable, Wi-Fi, or computer. You can also use the included On-the-Go adapter to transfer content quickly and easily from your old device.

1. From Settings, tap **Accounts and backup** > **Smart Switch**.

2. Follow the prompts and select the content to transfer.

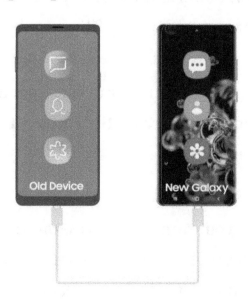

Note: Transferring content with a USB cable may increase battery consumption. Make sure your battery is fully charged

Lock or Unlock your Device

Use your device's screen lock features to secure your device. By default, the device locks automatically when the screen times out.

Side key
Press to lock.
Press to turn on the screen, and then swipe the screen to unlock it.

Side key settings

You can customize the shortcuts assigned to the Side key.

Double press

Choose which feature is launched when the Side key is pressed twice.

1. From Settings, tap **Advanced features** > **Side key**.

2. Tap **Double press** to enable this feature, and tap an option:

- Quick launch camera (default)
- Open Bixby|Open app

Press and hold

Choose which feature is launched when you press and hold the Side key.

1. From Settings, tap **Advanced features** > **Side key**.

2. Under the Press and hold heading, tap an option:

- Wake Bixby (default)
- Power off menu

Accounts

Set up and manage your accounts. **Tip:** Accounts may support email, calendars, contacts, and other features.

Add a Google Account

Sign in to your Google Account to access your Google Cloud Storage, apps installed from your account, and make full use of your device's Android™ features.

1. From Settings, tap **Accounts and backup** > **Accounts**

2. Tap **Add account** > **Google.**

Note: When you sign in to a Google Account, Factory Reset Protection (FRP) is activated. FRP requires your Google Account information when resetting to factory settings.

Add a Samsung

Account Sign in to your Samsung account to access exclusive Samsung content and make full use of Samsung apps.

1. From Settings, tap **Accounts and backup** > **Accounts.**

2. Tap **Add account** > **Samsung account.**

Tip: To quickly access your Samsung account, from Settings tap **Samsung account profile**.

Add an Outlook account

Sign in to your Outlook® account to view and manage email messages.

1. From Settings, tap 🔑 Accounts and backup > Accounts.

2. Tap ➕ Add account > Outlook

Set up voicemail

You can set up your voicemail service when you access it for the first time. You can access voicemail through the Phone app.

1. From 📞 **Phone**, touch and hold the ¹ **1 key**.

2. Follow the tutorial to create a password, record a greeting, and record your name.

Navigation

A touch screen responds best to a light touch from the pad of your finger or a capacitive stylus. Using excessive force or a metallic object on the touch screen may damage the tempered glass surface and void the warranty.

Tap

Lightly touch items to select or launch them.

- Tap an item to select it.
- Double-tap an image to zoom in or out.

Swipe

Lightly drag your finger across the screen.

- Swipe the screen to unlock the device.
- Swipe the screen to scroll through the Home screens or menu options.

Drag and drop

Touch and hold an item, and then move it to a new location.

- Drag an app shortcut to add it to a Home screen
- Drag a widget to place it in a new location.

Zoom in and out

Bring your thumb and forefinger together or apart to zoom in and out.

- Move your thumb and forefinger together on the screen to zoom out.
- Move your thumb and forefinger apart on the screen to zoom in.

Touch and hold

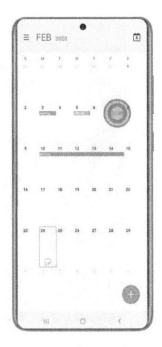

Touch and hold items to activate them.

- Touch and hold a field to display a pop-up Menu of options.
- Touch and hold a Home screen to customize the Home screen.

Navigation bar

You may navigate your device by using either the navigation buttons or full screen gestures.

Recent apps — Back

Home

Navigation buttons

Change how the navigation icons appear along the bottom of the screen.

- o From Settings, tap **Display** > **Navigation bar**. The following options are available:
  - **Navigation buttons**: Show the three navigation icons along the bottom of the screen.
  - **Button order**: Swap the order of the Back and Recent apps icons.

- **Full screen gestures**: Hide the navigation icons for an unobstructed screen experience, and use screen gestures to navigate. The following options are available:
  - **More options**: Configure additional options for Full screen gestures.
  - **Gesture hints**: Display lines at the bottom of the screen where each screen gesture is located.
  - **Show button to hide keyboard**: Show an icon on the bottom right corner of the screen to hide the keyboard when the phone is in portrait mode.

Full screen gestures options

Customize your Full screen gestures even further by adjusting the sensitivity and enabling different types of gestures.

  o From Settings, tap **Display** > **Navigation bar** > **Full screen gestures** > **More options** for the following:

- **Swipe from bottom**: Swipe up from three different areas at the bottom of the screen to go back, go to the Home screen, or view recent apps. You can also swipe up and hold the screen to use your device assistance app.
- **Swipe from sides and bottom**: Swipe inward from either side of the screen to go back, swipe up from the bottom of the screen to go to the Home screen, and swipe up and hold the screen to view your recent apps.
  - **Back gesture sensitivity**: Drag the slider to adjust your device's sensitivity to detecting back gestures.

Customize your home screen

The Home screen is the starting point for navigating your device. You can place your favorite apps and widgets here, in addition to setting up additional Home screens, removing screens, changing the order of screens, and choosing a main Home screen.

App icons

Use app icons to launch an app from any Home screen.

- From Apps, touch and hold an app icon, and tap Add to Home.

To remove an icon:

- From a Home screen, touch and hold an app icon, and then tap Remove from Home.

Note: Removing an icon does not delete the app; it just removes the icon from a Home screen.

Use folders

Organize App shortcuts in folders on an Apps screen or Home screen.

Wallpaper

Change the look of the Home and Lock screens by choosing a favorite picture, video, or preloaded wallpaper.

1. From a Home screen, touch and hold the screen, and then tap **Wallpaper**.

2. Tap one of the following menus for available wallpapers:

- **My wallpapers**: Choose from featured and downloaded wallpapers.

- **Gallery**: Choose pictures and videos saved in the Gallery app.

- **Wallpaper services**: Enable additional features including guide page and Dynamic Lock screen.

- **Apply Dark mode to Wallpaper**: Enable to apply Dark mode to your wallpaper.

- **Explore more wallpaper**: Find and download more wallpaper from Galaxy Themes.

3. Tap a picture or video to choose it.

    - If choosing a single picture, choose which screen or screens you want to apply the wallpaper to.

    - Videos and multiple pictures can only be applied to the Lock screen.

4. Tap Set on Home screen, Set on Lock screen, or Set on Home and Lock screens (depending on which screens are applicable).

    - If applying wallpaper to both the Home and Lock screens, enable Sync my edits if you want any edits made to that wallpaper to be applied to both screens.

Themes

Set a theme to be applied to your Home and Lock screens, wallpapers, and app icons.

1. From a Home screen, touch and hold the screen.
2. Tap **Themes to customize**.
3. Tap a theme to preview and download it to my themes.
4. Tap **My page** > **Themes** to see downloaded themes.
5. Tap a theme, and then tap Apply to apply the selected theme.

Icons

Apply different icon sets to replace the default icons.

1. From a Home screen, touch and hold the screen.
2. Tap **Themes** > **Icons to customize**.

3. Tap an icon set to preview and download it to my icons.

4. Tap 👤 **My page** > Icons to see downloaded icons.

5. Tap an icon, and then tap Apply to apply the selected icon set.

Widgets

Add widgets to your home screens for quick access to info or apps.

1. From a Home screen, touch and hold the screen.

2. Tap ▦ **Widgets** and then touch and hold a widget, drag it to a Home screen, and release it.

Customize Widgets

Once you have added a widget, you can customize where it's located and how it functions.

- From a Home screen, touch and hold a widget, and tap an option:

- **Remove from Home:** Delete a widget from your screen.

- **Widget settings:** Customize the function or appearance of the widget.

- **App info:** Review the widget usage, permissions, and more.

Home screen settings

Customize your Home and Apps screens.

1. From a Home screen, touch and hold the screen.

2. Tap Home screen settings to customize:

- **Home screen layout**: Set your device to have separate Home and Apps screens, or only a Home screen where all apps are located.

- **Home screen grid**: Choose a layout to determine how icons are arranged on the Home screen.

- **Apps screen grid**: Choose a layout to determine how icons are arranged on the Apps screen.

- **Apps button**: Add a button to the Home screen for easy access to the Apps screen.

- **App icon badges**: Enable to show badges on apps with active notifications. You can also choose the badge style.

- **Lock Home screen layout**: Prevent items on the Home screen from being removed or repositioned.

- **Add apps to Home screen**: Automatically add newly-downloaded apps to the Home screen.

- **Swipe down for notification panel**: Enable this feature to open the Notification panel by swiping down anywhere on the Home screen.

- **Rotate to landscape mode**: Rotate the Home screen automatically when your device's orientation is changed from portrait to landscape.

- **Hide apps**: Choose apps to hide from the Home and App screens. Return to this screen to restore hidden apps. Hidden apps are still installed and can appear as results in Finder searches.

- **About Home screen**: View version information

Easy mode

The Easy mode layout has larger text and icons, making for a more straightforward visual experience. Switch between the default screen layout and a simpler layout.

1. From Settings, tap **Display** > **Easy mode**.

2. Tap to enable this feature. The following options appear:

- Touch and hold delay: Set how long it takes for a continuous touch to be recognized as a touch and hold.

- High contrast keyboard: Choose a keyboard with high contrast colors.

To disable Easy mode:

1. From Settings, tap **Display** > **Easy mode**.

2. Tap to disable this feature.

Status bar

The Status bar provides device information on the right side and notification alerts on the left.

Status icons

Battery full   Battery low   Charging   Mute   Vibrate

Airplane mode   Bluetooth active   Wi-Fi active

Location active   Alarm Notification icons

Missed calls   call in progress   Call on hold

New message   Voicemail New email   Download

↑

Upload   Wi-Fi available   App update

Configure display options for the Status bar.

- o From Quick settings, tap ⋮ **More options** > **Status bar** for the following options:

- **Show notification icons**: Choose how to display notification icons on the Status bar.

- **Show battery percentage**: Display the battery charge percentage next to the battery icon on the Status bar.

Notification panel

For quick access to notifications, settings, and more, simply open the Notification panel.

View the Notification panel

You can access the Notification panel from any screen.

1. Drag the Status bar down to display the Notification panel.

2. Swipe down the list to see notification details.

- To open an item, tap it.

- To clear a single notification, drag the notification left or right.

- To clear all notifications, tap Clear.

- To customize notifications, **tap Notification settings**.

3. Drag upward from the bottom of the screen or tap ‹ **Back** to close the Notification panel.

Finger sensor gestures

You can also open or close the Notification panel by swiping up or down on the fingerprint sensor.

1. From Settings, tap **Advanced features** > **Motions and gestures** > **Finger sensor gestures**.

2. Tap to enable the feature.

Quick settings

The Notification panel also provides quick access to device functions using Quick settings.

1. Drag the Status bar down to display the Notification panel.

2. Drag — **View** all downward.

- Tap a quick setting icon to turn it on or off.

- Touch and hold a quick setting icon to open the setting.

- Tap **Finder search** to search the device.

- Tap **Power off** for Power off, Restart, and Emergency mode options.

- Tap **Open settings** to quickly access the device's settings menu.

- Tap **More options** to reorder Quick settings or to change the button layout.

3. Drag —**View** all upward to close Quick settings.

Samsung Daily

The Samsung Daily page displays customized content based on your interactions.

  o From a Home screen, swipe right.

Tip: You can add a Samsung Daily icon to your Apps list. Tap **More options** > **Settings** > **Add Samsung Daily icon.**

Customize Samsung Daily

Use the More options menu to add and reorder cards, customize settings, and learn how to use Samsung Daily.

1. From a Home screen, swipe right.

2. Tap ⋮ **More options** for the following options:

- **Cards**: Tap cards to add them to your Samsung Daily page.

- **Settings**: View the privacy policy, terms and conditions, and open source licensing and add a Samsung Daily icon to your Apps list.

- **Notices:** View Samsung Daily notices.

- **Tips:** Learn how to navigate Samsung Daily.

- **Help:** View FAQ and email customer service.

Bixby

Bixby is a virtual assistant that learns, evolves, and adapts to you.

It learns your routines, helps you set up reminders based on time and location, and is built in to your favorite apps.

   o From a Home screen, press and hold the Side key.

TIP: You can also access Bixby from the Apps list.

Bixby Routines

You can use Bixby to show you information or change device settings based on where you are and what you are doing.

- From Settings, tap **Advanced features > Bixby Routines.**

Bixby Vision

Bixby is integrated with your Camera, Gallery, and Internet apps to give you a deeper understanding of what you see. It provides contextual icons for translation, QR code detection, landmark recognition, or shopping.

Camera

Bixby Vision is available on the Camera viewfinder to help understand what you see.

- From **Camera**, tap **More > Bixby Vision** and follow the prompts.

Gallery

Bixby Vision can be used on pictures and images saved in the Gallery app.

1. From **Gallery,** tap a picture to view it.

2. Tap **Bixby Vision** and follow the prompts.

Internet

Bixby Vision can help you find out more about an image you find in the Internet app.

1. From **Internet,** touch and hold an image until a pop-up menu is displayed.

2. Tap **Bixby Vision** and follow the prompts.

Digital wellbeing and parental controls

You can monitor and manage your digital habits by getting a daily view of how frequently you use apps, how many notifications you receive, and how often you check your device. You can also set your device to help you wind down before going to bed.

- From Settings, tap **Digital wellbeing and parental controls** for the following features:

- **Screen time:** Tap the time value in the dashboard for details on how long each app has been opened and used today.

- **Notifications:** Tap to see how many notifications have been received from each app today.

- **Unlocks:** Tap to see how many times each app has been opened today.

- **Your goals:** Set up screen time and unlock goals and view your daily averages.

- **App timers:** Set a daily limit for how long you use each app.

- **Focus mode:** Configure times and activities to avoid distractions from your phone.

- **Wind down:** Enable to turn the screen to grayscale and limit notifications before going to bed.

- **Parental controls:** Supervise your children's digital life with Google's Family Link app. You can choose apps, set content filters, keep an eye on screen time, and set screen time limits.

Always On Display

View missed calls and message alerts, check the time and date, and view other customized information without unlocking your device using Always on Display (AOD).

1. From Settings, tap 🔒 **Lock screen > Always on Display.**

2. Tap to enable the feature, and then set the following options:

- Choose when to show a clock and notifications on the screen when your device is not in use: **Tap to show, Show always, or Show as scheduled.**

- **Clock style:** Change the style and color options for the clock on the Lock screen and Always on Display.

- **Show music information:** Show music details when the FaceWidgets music controller is in use.

- **Rotate screen to:** Display the AOD in portrait or landscape mode.

- **Auto brightness:** Automatically adjust the brightness of Always on Display.

- **About Always On Display:** View the current software version and license information.

Note: Some display settings can appear on both the Lock screen and Always On Display

AOD themes

Apply custom themes for Always on Display.

1. From a Home screen, touch and hold the screen, and tap **Themes > AODs.**

    - Tap an AOD to preview and download it to My Always on Displays.

2. Tap **My page > AODs** to see downloaded AODs.

3. Tap an AOD, and then tap **Apply.**

Biometric security

Use biometrics to securely unlock your device and log in to accounts.

Face recognition

You can enable Face Recognition to unlock your screen. To use your face to unlock your device, you must set a pattern, PIN, or password.

- Face recognition is less secure than Pattern, PIN, or Password. Your device could be unlocked by someone or something that looks like your image.

- Some conditions may affect face recognition, including wearing glasses, hats, beards, or heavy make-up.

- When registering your face, ensure that you are in a well-lit area and the camera lens is clean.

1. From Settings, tap **Biometrics and security > Face recognition.**

2. Follow the prompts to register your face.

Face recognition management

Customize how face recognition works.

- ○ From Settings, tap **Biometrics and security > Face recognition.**

- **Remove face data:** Delete existing faces.

- **Add alternative look**: Enhance face recognition by adding an alternative appearance.

- **Face unlock:** Enable or disable face recognition security.

- **Stay on Lock screen**: When you unlock your device with face recognition, stay on the Lock screen until you swipe the screen.

- **Faster recognition**: Turn on for faster face recognition. Turn off to increase security and make it harder to unlock using an image or video of your likeness.

- **Require open eyes**: Facial recognition will only recognize your face when your eyes are open.

- Brighten screen: Increase the screen brightness temporarily so that your face can be recognized in dark conditions.

- Samsung Pass: Access your online accounts using face recognition.

- About unlocking with biometrics: Learn additional information about securing your device with biometrics.

Fingerprint scanner

Use fingerprint recognition as an alternative to entering passwords in certain apps. You can also use your fingerprint to verify your identity when logging in to your Samsung account. To use your fingerprint to unlock your device, you must set a pattern, PIN, or password.

1. From Settings, tap **Biometrics and security > Fingerprints**.

2. Follow the prompts to register your fingerprint.

Fingerprint management

Add, delete, and rename fingerprints.

- ○ From Settings, tap **Biometrics and security > Fingerprints** for the following options:

- The list of registered fingerprints is at the top of this list. You can tap a fingerprint to remove or rename it.

- **Add fingerprint**: Simply follow the prompts to register another fingerprint.

- **Check added fingerprints**: Scan your fingerprint to see if it has been registered.

Fingerprint verification settings

Use fingerprint recognition to verify your identity in supported apps and actions.

- ○ From Settings, tap **Biometrics and security > Fingerprints.**

- **Fingerprint unlock**: Use your fingerprint for identification when unlocking your device.

- **Fingerprint always on**: Wake and unlock your device by just touching the Power key.

- **Samsung Pass**: Use your fingerprint for identification when using supported apps.

- **About unlocking with biometrics**: Read details on the requirements each biometric security feature has for using your pattern, PIN, or password as a backup.

Biometrics preferences

Configure your preferences for biometric security options.

- o From Settings, tap **Biometrics and security > Biometrics preferences** for the following:

- Screen transition effect: Show a transition effect when you use biometrics to unlock your device.

Note: From Settings, tap **Biometrics and security > Biometrics security patch** to view the software version of your device's biometric security features.

Mobile continuity

Phone calls, messages, photo and video storage, and other functions of your device can be accessed and integrated across compatible mobile devices and computers.

Link to Windows

Achieve mobile continuity between your Samsung device and Windows-based PCs. Get instant access to your device's photos, messages, and more on a PC by linking your devices.

Pictures

- Drag and drop pictures to Windows.
- Open and edit pictures in the Your Photos app.
- Share images with your contacts through Windows.

Messages (SMS/MMS)

- MMS group messaging support.
- Integration with Windows Emoji Picker.
- Get a Windows pop-up when receiving a new message.

Notifications

- See and manage phone notifications from your PC.

- Exclude notifications from individual phone apps.
- Get a Windows pop-up when receiving a new notification.

App mirroring

- Live stream your phone screen on your PC.
- Interact with your phone using the keyboard and mouse.
- Use Windows Accessibility.

Link your device to your computer

1. From Settings, tap **Advanced features > Link to Windows.**
2. Tap to enable this feature.
3. Follow the prompts to connect your device to your PC.

Tip: You can also enable this feature from the Quick settings menu.

Call & text on other devices

This feature allows you to make and answer calls and text messages from your Galaxy devices that are signed in to your Samsung account.

1. From Settings, tap **Advanced features** > **Call & text on other devices**.

2. Tap to turn on the feature. Connection occurs automatically.

3. Sign in to your Samsung account on your Galaxy devices.

Tip: Move your contacts from your phone to your Samsung account so you can access them on all registered devices.

Multi window

Multitask by using multiple apps at the same time. Apps that support Multi window™ can be displayed together on a split screen. You can switch between the apps and adjust the size of their windows.

Split screen control

1. From any screen, tap ||| **Recent apps**.

2. Tap the app icon, and then tap Open in split screen view.

3. Tap an app in the other window to add it to the split screen view.

    - Drag the middle of the window border to adjust the window size.

Multi window Tray

The Multi window tray is a shortcut to apps that are compatible with Multi window.

1. From an app, swipe the handle at the edge of the screen to access the Multi window tray.

2. Tap an app to open it in Multi window.

Tip: You can customize the Multi window tray. From Settings, tap **Advanced features** > **Multi window tray**.

Edge screen

The Edge screen is made up of several customizable edge panels. Edge panels can be used to access apps, tasks, and contacts, as well as view news, sports, and other information.

Edge handle

Apps panel

You can add up to ten apps in two columns to the Apps panel.

1. From any screen, drag the Edge handle to the center of the screen. Swipe until the Apps panel is displayed.
2. Tap an app or app pair to open it.

To configure Apps panel:

1. From any screen, drag the Edge handle to the center of the screen. Swipe until the Apps panel is displayed.
2. Tap ⊕ Add apps to folder to add other apps to the Apps panel.
   - To add an app to the Apps panel, find it on the left side of the screen and tap it to add it to an available space on the right column.
   - To create a shortcut for two apps to open in Multi window, tap Create app pair.

- To create a folder shortcut, drag an app from the left side of the screen on top of an app in the columns on the right.

- To change the order of the apps on the panel, drag each app to the desired location.

- To remove an app, tap ▬ Remove.

3. Tap ＜ Back to save changes.

Smart Select

The Smart select feature captures an area of the screen as an image or animation that you can share or pin to the screen.

1. From any screen, drag the Edge handle to the center of the screen. Swipe until the Smart select panel is displayed.
2. Tap a Smart select tool to use:

  - ▢ Rectangle: Capture a rectangular area of the screen.

  - ◯ Oval: Capture an oval area of the screen.

- **Animation**: Record activity on the screen as an animated GIF.

- **Pin to screen**: Capture an area and pin it to the screen.

Tools

The Tools panel provides handy instruments for quick access.

1. From any screen, drag the Edge handle to the center of the screen. Swipe until the Tools panel is displayed.
2. Tap a tool to use:

- **Compass**: Identify compass directions.

    – Tap Calibrate to calibrate the compass.

- **Tally counter**: Use the plus and minus icons to add or subtract while counting.

    – Tap Vibration to enable or disable vibrations with each addition or subtraction.

    – Tap Target to set a total target number between 1 and 9999.

– Tap ⟳ Reset to reset the counter.

- Flashlight: Tap 🔦 Flashlight to turn the flashlight on and off. Use the plus and minus icons to increase or decrease the brightness of the light.

    – Tap SOS to make the flashlight signal the phrase "SOS" in Morse code.

- Surface level: Use the device to determine if a surface is level by placing the device on the surface. The surface is level when the x and y values are close to or equal to zero degrees.

    – Tap Calibrate to calibrate the level.

- Ruler: Use the edge of the device as a ruler to measure a straight line in either inches or centimeters. Tap the unit name to change the units.

Configure Edge panels

You can customize the Edge panels.

1. From the Edge screen, tap ⚙ Settings.

2. Tap ⬤ to enable the feature. The following options are available:

- ✓ Checkbox: Enable or disable each panel.
- Edit (if available): Configure individual panels.
- 🔍 Search: Find panels that are either installed or available to install.
- More options:
    - Reorder: Change the order of the panels by dragging them to the left or right.
    - Uninstall: Remove an Edge panel from your device.
    - Handle settings: Customize the position and style of the Edge handle.
- Galaxy Store: Search for and download more Edge panels from Galaxy Store.

Tap ‹ Back to save changes.

Edge panel position

You can change the position of the Edge handle.

1. From the Edge screen, tap ⚙ Settings.
2. Tap ⋮ More options > Handle settings for the following options:

   - ⬍ Edge handle: Drag to change the position of the Edge handle along the edge of the screen.
   - Position: Choose either Right or Left to set which side the Edge screen displays on.
   - Lock handle position: Enable to prevent the handle position from being moved when touched and held.

Edge panel style

Change the style of the Edge handle.

1. From the Edge screen, tap ⚙ Settings.
2. Tap ⋮ More options > Handle settings for the following options:

   - Colors: Choose a color for the Edge handle.
   - Transparency: Drag the slider to adjust the transparency of the Edge handle.

- Size: Drag the slider to adjust the size of the Edge handle.

Edge lighting

Set the Edge screen to light up when you receive calls or notifications, which makes alerts visible even when the screen is face-down.

1. From Settings, tap Display > Edge screen > Edge lighting.
2. Tap to enable the feature.

Lighting style

Customize the color, width, and transparency of the Edge lighting feature.

1. From Settings, tap ⚙ Display > Edge screen > Edge lighting.
2. Tap Lighting style to customize:

- Effect: Choose an edge effect.
- Color: Choose a preset or custom color, and enable app colors.
    - Tap Add keyword to configure a custom lighting effect for specific text that appears in notification titles.
- Advanced: Adjust other Edge lighting qualities.
    - Transparency: Drag the slider to adjust the transparency of the Edge lighting.
    - Width: Drag the slider to adjust the width of the Edge lighting.
    - Duration: Drag the slider to adjust how short or long the Edge lighting displays.

3. Tap Done when finished.

Choose apps

Choose which apps activate Edge lighting.

  1. From Settings, tap Display > Edge screen > Edge lighting.
  2. Tap Choose apps to choose the apps that can activate Edge lighting when a notification is received.

Show Edge lighting

Choose when Edge lighting will replace notifications.

  1. From Settings, tap Display > Edge screen > Edge lighting.
  2. Tap Show Edge lighting to choose:
     - While screen is on: Edge lighting will replace regular notification pop-ups.
     - While screen is off: Edge lighting will replace notifications that turn the screen on.
     - Always: Display edge lighting for all notifications regardless of if the screen is on or off.

About Edge screen

You can view the current software version and license information for the Edge screen feature.

- From Settings, tap Display > Edge screen > About Edge screen.

Enter text

Text can be entered using a keyboard or your voice.

Toolbar functions

The toolbar provides additional helpful functions.

- From the Samsung keyboard, tap Expand toolbar for the following options:

- **Bitmoji:** Create your own personal emoji and use it in stickers.

- **Clipboard:** Access the clipboard.

- **Emojis:** Insert an emoji.

- **GIF keyboard**: Add animated GIFs.

- **Keyboard size:** Adjust the height and width of the keyboard.

- **Modes:** Select a keyboard layout.

- **Mojitok:** Create your own stickers or insert automatically suggested ones.

- **My Emoji:** Create your own personal emoji and use it in stickers you can share.

- **Samsung Pass:** Use biometrics for secure access to apps and services.

- **Settings:** Access keyboard settings.

- **Stickers:** Add illustrated stickers.

- **Translate:** Type words or sentences in the keyboard to translate them into another language.

- **Spotify:** Add music from Spotify.

- **Search:** Locate specific words or phrases in your conversations.

- **Text editing:** Use an editing panel to help pinpoint text that you want to cut, copy, and paste.

- **Voice input:** Use Samsung voice input.

Configure the Samsung keyboard

Set customized options for the Samsung keyboard.

- o From the Samsung keyboard, Tap **Settings** for the following options:

- **Languages and types:** Set the keyboard type and choose which languages are available on the keyboard.

- To switch between languages, swipe the Space bar left or right.

- **Smart typing:** Use predictive text and auto-correction features to prevent common typing mistakes. Type by swiping between letters.

- Style and layout: Customize the appearance and function of the keyboard.

- Swipe, touch, and feedback: Customize gestures and feedback.

- Reset to default settings: Return keyboard to original settings and clear personalized data.

- **About Samsung keyboard**: View version and legal information for the Samsung keyboard.

Use Samsung voice input

Instead of typing, enter text by speaking.

o From the Samsung keyboard, tap **Voice input** and speak your text

Configure Samsung voice input

Set customized options for Samsung voice input.

1. From the Samsung keyboard, tap **Voice input.**

2. Tap **Settings** for options.

- Keyboard language: Choose the language for the keyboard.

- Voice input language: Select the language for Samsung voice input.

- Hide offensive words: Hide potentially offensive words with asterisks.

- About Samsung voice input: View version and legal information for Samsung voice input.

Emergency mode

Use Emergency mode to access helpful emergency features and conserve your device's power during an emergency situation.

To save battery power, Emergency mode:

- Restricts application usage to only essential applications and those you select.

- Turns off connectivity features and Mobile data when the screen is off.

Activate Emergency mode

To activate Emergency mode:

1. Open the Notification panel, and tap ⏻ **Power.**

2. Tap 🛑 **Emergency mode.**

    - When accessing for the first time, read and accept the terms and conditions.

3. Tap Turn on.

Emergency mode features

While in Emergency mode, only the following apps and features are available on the Home screen:

- **Flashlight:** Use the device's flash as a steady source of light.

- **Emergency alarm:** Sound an audible siren.

- **Share my location:** Send your location information to your emergency contacts.

- **Phone:** Launch the call screen.

- **Internet:** Launch the web browser.

- ⊕ **Add**

 - **Calculator:** Launch the Calculator app.

 - **Clock:** Launch the Clock app. – Maps: Launch Google Maps™.

 - **Outlook:** Launch the Outlook app.

 - **Samsung Notes:** Launch the Samsung Notes app.

- **Battery charge:** Displays estimated battery charge percentage.

- **Estimated battery life:** Displays estimated remaining battery charge time based on current battery charge and usage.

- **Emergency call:** Dial the emergency telephone number (for example, 911). This kind of call can be made even without activated service.

- ⋮ **More options:**

 - **Turn off Emergency mode:** Disable Emergency mode and return to standard mode.

- **Remove apps:** Choose apps to remove from the screen.

- **Emergency contacts:** Manage your medical profile and ICE (In Case of Emergency) group contacts.

- **Settings:** Configure the available settings. Only a limited number of settings are enabled in Emergency mode.

Turn off Emergency mode

When emergency mode is turned off, the device returns to standard mode.

- Tap **More options**, and tap **Turn off Emergency mode.**

Note: When Emergency mode is activated, Locating method is set to Battery saving. After Emergency mode is turned off, you may need to adjust your location settings.

Chapter 3
Camera and Gallery

You can capture high-quality pictures and videos using the Camera app. Images and videos are stored in the Gallery, where you can view and edit them.

Camera

Enjoy a full kit of pro lenses and pro-grade video modes and settings.

- From Apps, tap **Camera.**

Tip: If Quick launch is enabled, quickly press the **Side** key twice.

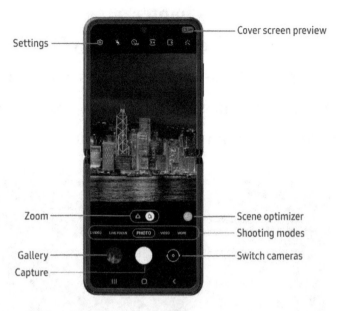

Navigate the camera screen

Take stunning pictures with your device's front and rear cameras.

1. From **Camera**, set up your shot with the following features:

- Tap the screen where you want the camera to focus.
- When you tap the screen, a brightness scale appears. Drag the circle to adjust the brightness.
- To quickly switch between the front and rear cameras, swipe the screen up or down.

- To change to a different shooting mode, swipe the screen right or left.

- To change camera settings, tap **Settings.**

2. Tap Capture.

Configure shooting mode

Allow the camera to determine the ideal mode for your pictures or choose from several shooting modes.

- From **Camera**, swipe the screen right and left to change shooting modes.

  - **Photo:** Allow the camera to determine the ideal settings for pictures.

  - **Video:** Allow the camera to determine the ideal settings for videos.

  - **Live focus:** Take artistic pictures by adjusting the depth of field.

  - **Live focus video:** Record artistic videos with adjustable depths of focus.

  - **More:** Choose other available shooting modes. Tap **Edit** to drag modes into or out of the Modes tray at the bottom of the Camera screen.

- **Pro:** Manually adjust the ISO sensitivity, exposure value, white balance, and color tone while taking pictures.

- **Panorama:** Create a linear image by taking pictures in either a horizontal or vertical direction.

- **Food:** Take pictures that emphasize the vivid colors of food.

- **Night:** Use this to take photos in low-light conditions, without using the flash.

- **Super slow-mo:** Record videos at an extremely high frame rate for viewing in high quality slow motion. You can play a specific section of each video in slow motion after recording it.

- **Slow motion:** Record videos at a high frame rate for viewing in slow motion.

- **Hyperlapse:** Create a time lapse video by recording at various frame rates. The frame rate is adjusted depending on the scene being recorded and the movement of the device.

- **Pro video:** Manually adjust the ISO sensitivity, exposure value, white balance, and color tone while recording videos.

AR Zone

Access all of your Augmented Reality (AR) features in one place.

- From ⌾ **Camera**, swipe to **More,** and then tap **AR Zone.** The following features are available:
- **AR Emoji Camera:** Use the camera to create your My Emoji avatar.
- **AR Doodle:** Enhance videos by adding line drawings or handwriting to your environment. AR Doodle tracks faces and space so they move with you.
- **AR Emoji Studio:** Use AR tools to create and customize your My Emoji avatar.
- **AR Emoji Stickers:** Add AR stickers to your My Emoji avatar.
- **Deco Pic:** Decorate photos or videos in real time with the camera.

- **Makeup:** Preview makeup styles using the camera.
- **Styling:** Try on sunglasses using the camera.

Live focus

Add interactive focus effects to your pictures.

1. From ◉ **Camera**, swipe to **Live focus**.
2. Tap ◉ **Live focus effect**, choose an effect, and drag the slider to fine-tune the effect

Scene optimizer

Automatically adjust exposure, contrast, white balance, and more based on what is detected in the camera frame to help you capture beautiful photos.

- From ◉ **Camera,** swipe to Photo, and tap ❈ **Scene optimizer.**

Note: The Scene optimizer is only available when using the rear camera. The Scene optimizer icon will change automatically based on what the camera detects, such as ❀ when taking nature photos or ☾ when taking photos in a dark setting.

Record videos

Record high-quality videos using your device.

1. From 📷 **Camera**, swipe right or left to change the shooting mode to **Video**.

2. Tap ● **Capture** to begin recording a video.

   - To take a picture while recording, tap 📷 **Capture**.

   - To temporarily stop recording, tap ‖ **Pause**. To continue recording, tap ● **Resume**.

3. Tap ■ **Stop** when you are finished recording.

Live focus video

Create professional-looking films by applying background blurs and other special effects to your video. This feature cannot be used with zoom, Zoom-in mic, or Super steady.

1. From 📷 **Camera**, swipe to **Live focus video.**

2. Tap ⊙ **Live focus effect**, choose an effect, and drag the slider to fine-tune the effect.

3. Tap ● **Capture** to begin recording.

Super Slow-mo

Record videos at a high frame rate for viewing in slow motion.

1. From 📷 **Camera**, swipe to **More,** and then tap **Super slow-mo.**

2. Tap **Super Slow-mo** to record.

Tip: Hold your device steady for best results.

Super steady

Super steady applies advanced stabilization algorithms to your video for a smooth, professional appearance, even in heavy motion situations. This feature cannot be used with Zoom-in mic, Live focus video, Slow motion, or the front camera.

1. From 📷 **Camera**, swipe to change the shooting mode to **Video.**

2. Tap **Super steady**.

3. Tap **Capture** to begin recording.

Camera settings

Use the icons on the main camera screen and the settings menu to configure your camera's settings.

- From 📷 Camera, tap ⚙️ **Settings** for the following options: **Intelligent features**

  - **Scene optimizer:** Automatically adjust the color settings of your pictures to match the subject matter.

  - **Shot suggestions:** Get tips to help you choose the best shooting mode.

  - **Smart selfie angle:** Automatically switch to a wide-angle selfie when there are more than two people in the frame.

  - **Scan QR codes:** Automatically detect QR codes when using the camera.

Pictures

  - **Swipe Shutter button to edge to:** Choose to either take a burst shot or create a GIF when you swipe the shutter to the nearest edge.

  - **Save options:** Choose file formats and other saving options.

- **HEIF pictures (Photo):** Save pictures as high efficiency images to save space. Some sharing sites may not support this format.

- **Save RAW copies:** Save JPEG and RAW copies of pictures taken in Pro mode.

- **Ultra wide shape correction:** Automatically correct distortion in pictures taken with the ultra wide lens.

Videos

- **Rear video size:** Select a resolution. Selecting a higher resolution for higher quality requires more memory.

- **Front video size:** Select a resolution. Selecting a higher resolution for higher quality requires more memory.

- **Advanced recording options:** Enhance your videos with advanced recording formats.

  - **High efficiency video:** Record videos in HEVC format to save space. Other devices or sharing sites may not support playback of this format.

- **HDR10+ video:** Optimize videos by recording in HDR10+. Playback devices must support HDR10+ video.

- **Video stabilization:** Activate anti-shake to keep the focus steady when the camera is moving.

Useful features

- **Auto HDR:** Capture more detail in the bright and dark areas of your shots.

- **Tracking auto-focus:** Keep a moving subject in focus.

- **Pictures as previewed:** Save selfies as they appear in the preview without flipping them.

- **Grid lines:** Display viewfinder grid lines to help compose a picture or video.

- **Location tags:** Attach a GPS location tag to the picture.

Shooting methods:

- **Press Volume key to**: Use the Volume key to take pictures, record video, zoom, or control system volume.

- **Voice control**: Take pictures speaking key words.

- **Floating shutter button**: Add an extra shutter button that you can move anywhere on the screen.

- **Show palm**: Hold your hand out with your palm facing the camera to have your picture taken in a few seconds.

- **Tabletop layout**: Split the screen into top and bottom halves when the phone is folded upright.

- **Shutter sound**: Play a tone when taking a picture.

- **Reset settings**: Reset the camera settings.

- **About Camera**: View app and software information.

Gallery

Go to the Gallery to look at the all the visual media stored on your device. You can view, edit, and manage pictures and videos.

- From Apps, tap **Gallery.**

View pictures

Pictures stored on your device are viewable in the Gallery app.

1. From ✴ **Gallery**, tap **Pictures.**

2. Tap a picture to view it. Swipe left or right to view other pictures or videos.

- To use Bixby Vision on the current picture, tap 👁 **Bixby Vision**.

- To mark the picture as a favorite, tap ♡ **Favorite.**

- To access the following features, tap ⋮ **More options:**

- **Details**: View and edit information about the picture.

- **Set as wallpaper**: Set the picture as wallpaper.

- **Set as Always On Display image**: Set the picture as the background image for the Always On Display.

- **Move to Secure Folder**: Move the picture to a Secure Folder.

- **Print**: Send the picture to a connected printer.

Edit pictures

Enhance your pictures using the Gallery's editing tools.

1. From Gallery, tap Pictures.

2. Tap a picture to view it, and then tap Edit for the following options:

- Transform: Rotate, flip, crop, or make other changes to the overall appearance of the picture.

- Filters: Add color effects.

- Tone: Adjust the brightness, exposure, contrast, and more.

- Sticker: Overlay illustrated or animated stickers.

- **T** Text: Add text to the picture.

- 🎨 Draw: Add handwritten text or hand drawn content.

3. Tap Save when finished.

Play video

View the videos stored on your device. You can save videos as favorites, and view video details.

1. From **Gallery,** tap Pictures.

2. Tap a video to view it. Swipe left or right to view other pictures or videos.

- To mark the video as a favorite, tap ♡ **Favorite.** The video is added to Favorites under the Albums tab.

- To access the following features, tap ⋮ **More options:**

 – **Details**: View and edit information about the video.

 – **Set as wallpaper**: Set the video as wallpaper on the Lock screen.

 – **Move to Secure Folder**: Add this video to your Secure Folder.

3. Tap ▶ **Play** video to play the video.

Video enhancer

Enhance the image quality of your videos to enjoy brighter and more vivid colors.

1. From **Settings,** tap Advanced features > Video enhancer.

2. Tap to enable this feature.

Edit video

Edit videos stored on your device.

1. From **Gallery**, tap **Pictures**.

2. Tap a video to view it.

3. Tap **Edit** to use the following tools:

- **Rotate**: Rotate the video clockwise.

- **Trim**: Cut segments of the video.

- **Filters**: Add visual effects to the video.

- **Portrait**: Enhance skin tones, eyes, and other facial features.

- **Text**: Add text to your videos.

- **Sticker**: Overlay illustrated or animated stickers.

- **Draw**: Draw on your video.

- **Speed**: Adjust the play speed.

- **Audio**: Adjust the volume levels and add background music to the video.

4. Tap Save, and then confirm when prompted.

Share pictures and videos

Share pictures and videos from the Gallery app.

1. From **Gallery**, tap **Pictures**.

2. Tap **More options** > **Share**, and then tap pictures and videos to select them.

3. Tap **Share**, and then choose an app or connection to use for sharing your selection. Follow the prompts.

Delete pictures and videos

Delete pictures and videos stored on your device.

1. From **Gallery**, tap **More options** > **Edit**.

2. Tap pictures and videos to select them, or tap the All checkbox at the top of the screen to select all pictures and videos.

3. Tap 🗑 **Delete**, and confirm when prompted.

Create movie

Share pictures and videos from the Gallery app by creating a slideshow of your content with video effects and music.

1. From ✱ **Gallery**, tap 🎬 **Create movie.**

2. Tap pictures and videos to add them to the movie.

3. Tap 🎬 **Create movie** and then choose either **Highlight reel** (automatic slideshow) or **Self-edited** (custom slideshow). The following options are available:

- ⏱ **Duration**: Adjust the run time of the entire movie (Highlight reel only).

- ▭ **Transition effect**: Add visual interest to your movie by customizing the transitions between each clip (Self-edited only).

- **Title**: Add a title and a description to your movie.

- **Audio**: Adjust the volume of your movie, add sounds effects, or add music

- **Clips**: View and edit each video or picture in your movie.

- **Add**: Incorporate additional clips from the gallery (Self-edited only).

- **Share**: Send your movie to friends and family.

4. Tap **Save.**

Take a screenshot

Capture an image of your screen. Your device will automatically create a Screenshots album in the Gallery app.

- o From any screen, press and release the **Side** and **Volume down** keys.

Screen recorder

Record activities on your device, write notes, and use the camera to record a video overlay of yourself to share with friends or family.

1. From Quick Settings, tap **Screen recorder** to begin recording.

- Tap **Draw** to draw on the screen.

- Tap **Selfie video** to include a recording from your front camera.

2. Tap **Stop** to finish recording. These are automatically saved to the Screen recording album in the Gallery.

Screen recorder settings

Control the sound and quality settings for the screen recorder.

o From Settings, tap **Advanced features** > **Screenshots and screen recorder** > **Screen recorder settings.**

- **Sound**: Choose what sounds to record while using the screen recorder.

- **Video quality**: Select a resolution. Selecting a higher resolution for higher quality requires more memory.

- **Selfie video size**: Drag the slider to set the size of the video overlay.

Chapter 4
Using Apps

Download apps

The Apps list displays all preloaded and downloaded apps. Apps can be downloaded from Galaxy Store and the Google Play™ store.

- From a Home screen, swipe the screen upward to access the Apps list.

Uninstall or disable apps

Installed apps can be removed from your device. Some apps that are preloaded (available on your device by default) can only be disabled. Disabled apps are turned off and hidden from the Apps list.

- From Apps, touch and hold an app, and tap Uninstall/Disable.

Search for apps

If you are not sure where to find an app or a setting, you can use the Search feature.

1. From Apps, tap Search, and enter a word or words. As you type, matching apps and settings appear as results on the screen.

2. Tap a result to go to that app.

Tip: You can customize the search settings by tapping **More options** > **Finder settings**.

Sort apps

App shortcuts can be listed alphabetically or in your own custom order.

- From Apps, tap **More options** > **Sort** for the following sorting options:
    - **Custom order**: Arrange apps manually.
    - **Alphabetical order**: Sort apps alphabetically.

Tip: When apps are arranged manually (Custom order), empty icon spaces can be removed by tapping **More options** > **Clean up pages.**

Create and use folders

You can make folders to organize App shortcuts on the Apps list.

1. From Apps, touch and hold an app shortcut, and then drag it on top of another app shortcut until it is highlighted.

2. Release the app shortcut to create the folder.

- **Folder name**: Name the folder.

- **Palette**: Change the folder color.

- Add apps: Place more apps in the folder. Tap apps to select them, and then tap **Done.**

3. Tap **Back** to close the folder.

Copy a folder to a Home screen

You can copy a folder to a Home screen.

- o From Apps, touch and hold a folder, and tap **Add to Home.**

Delete a folder

When you delete a folder, the app shortcuts return to the Apps list.

1. From Apps, touch and hold a folder to delete.

2. Tap **Delete folder**, and confirm when prompted.

Game Booster

Get optimized performance while playing games based on usage. Block calls or other notifications, and enable features such as Bixby or Dolby Atmos.

- o While playing a game, swipe up from the bottom of the screen to view the navigation bar. The following options are seen on the far right and left sides:

  - **Screen touch lock**: Lock the screen to prevent accidental taps. This is the default option.

  - **Game Booster**: Configure other options, including performance monitoring and blocking the navigation bar, screen touches, and screenshots.

App settings

Manage your downloaded and preloaded apps. Options vary by app.

1. From Settings, tap Apps.

2. Tap **More options** for the following options:

- **Sort by**: Sort the apps by size, name, last used, or last updated.

- **Default apps**: Choose or change apps that are used by default for certain features, like email or browsing the Internet.

- **Permission manager**: Control which apps have permissions to use certain features of your device.

- **Show/Hide system apps**: Show or hide system (background) apps.

- **Special access**: Select which apps can have special access permissions to features on your device.

- **Reset app preferences**: Reset options that have been changed. Existing app data is not deleted.

3. Tap an app to view and update information about the app. The following options may be displayed:

Usage

• **Mobile data**: View mobile data usage.

• **Battery**: View battery usage since the last full charge.

• **Storage**: Manage the app's storage usage.

• **Memory**: View memory usage.

App settings

- **Notifications**: Configure notifications from the app.

- **Permissions**: View permissions granted to the app for access to your device's information.

- **Set as default**: Set the app as a default for a certain category of apps.

Advanced

- Options vary by app.

App info options

- **Open**: Launch the app. Not all apps have this option.

- **Uninstall/Disable**: Uninstall or disable the app. Some preloaded apps can only be disabled, not uninstalled.

- **Force stop**: Stop an app that is not working correctly.

Samsung apps

The following apps are either preloaded or downloaded over-the-air to your device during setup.

Galaxy Essentials

Galaxy Essentials is a collection of specially chosen applications available through Samsung apps. You can access and download a collection of premium content.

- From Apps, tap **More options** > **Galaxy Essentials**.

AR Zone

Access all of your Augmented Reality (AR) features in one place

- From Apps, tap Samsung folder > **AR Zone**.

Bixby

Bixby displays customized content based on your interactions. Bixby learns from your usage patterns and suggests content you may like.

- From Apps, tap Samsung folder > **Bixby**.

Galaxy Store

Find and download premium apps that are exclusive to Galaxy devices. A Samsung account is required to download from Galaxy Store.

- From Apps, tap **Galaxy Store**.

Galaxy Wearable

Connect your device to your Samsung Watch using this application.

- From Apps, tap Samsung folder > **Galaxy Wearable.**

Game Launcher

Automatically arrange all your games in one place.

- From Apps, tap **Game Launcher**.

Tip: If Game Launcher is not seen in the Apps list, then from Settings, tap **Advanced features** > **Game Launcher**, and then tap.

Samsung Global Goals

Learn more about the Global Goals initiative and contribute towards donations that support these causes with ads from this app.

- From Apps, tap Samsung Global Goals.

Samsung Members

Get more and do more from your Galaxy device. Enjoy DIY support tools and exclusive experiences and content — for

Samsung members only. Samsung Members may be preloaded on your device, or you can download and install it from Galaxy Store or the Google Play store.

- From Apps, tap Samsung Members.

SmartThings

SmartThings allows you to control, automate, and monitor your home environment through a mobile device to fit your specific needs. You can use the app to connect multiple devices at once or one device at a time. Check the status of your devices by looking at the dashboard.

- From Apps, tap **Samsung** folder > **SmartThings,** and sign in with your Samsung account.

Note: Non-Samsung connected device errors or defects are not covered by the Samsung warranty; contact the non-Samsung device manufacturer for support.

Tips:

View tips and techniques as well as the user manual for your device.

o   From Apps, tap **Samsung** folder >  **Tip**

Calculator

The Calculator app features both basic and scientific math functions, as well as a unit converter.

o   From Apps, tap   Calculator

Unit converter
Convert between measurements.

History
View past calculations.

Scientific mode
If the icon is not visible, turn your device to landscape.

Calendar

The Calendar app can be connected to your various online accounts to consolidate all your calendars in one place.

o   From Apps, tap   Calendar.

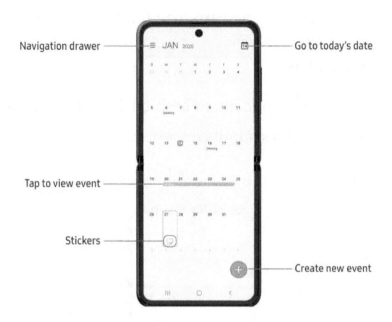

Add calendars

Add your accounts to the Calendar app.

1. From Calendar, tap ☰ **Navigation drawer**.

2. Tap **Settings** > **Add new account** and select an account type.

3. Enter your account information and follow the prompts.

Tip: Accounts may also support email, contacts, and other features.

Subscription calendars

Subscribe to calendars that match your interests, you can easily find a variety of upcoming events and add them to your schedule.

1. From **Calendar**, tap **Navigation drawer**.

2. Tap Subscribe to your interests and follow the prompts.

Calendar alert style

Alerts from the Calendar app can be set to different styles.

1. From **Calendar**, tap **Navigation drawer** > **Settings** > **Alert style**. The following options are available:

    - **Light**: Receive a notification and hear a short sound.

    - **Medium**: Get a full screen alert and hear a short sound.

    - **Strong**: Get a full-screen alert and ring sound that persist until dismissed.

2. Depending on the alert style selected above, the following sound options are available:

- **Ring once sound**: Choose the alert sound for Light or Medium alert styles.

- **Keep ringing sound**: Choose the alert sound for the Strong alert style.

Create an event

Use your Calendar to create events.

1. From 🗓 **Calendar**, tap ➕ **Add event** to add an event.

2. Enter details for the event, and then tap **Save**.

Delete an event

Delete events from your Calendar.

1. From 🗓 **Calendar**, tap an event, and tap again to edit it.

2. Tap 🗑 **Delete**, and confirm when prompted

🕐 Clock

The Clock app offers features for keeping track of time and setting alarms.

- From Apps, tap 🕐 Clock, and tap a tab to use a feature

Alarm

Use the Alarm tab to set one-time or recurring alarms and choose options for how to be notified.

1. From ⏰ **Clock**, tap ➕ **Add alarm**.
2. Tap the following items to configure an alarm:

    - **Time**: Set a time for the alarm.
    - **Day**: Choose the days for this alarm.
    - **Alarm name**: Enter a name for the alarm.

- **Alarm sound**: Choose a sound to play for the alarm and drag the slider to set the volume of the alarm.

- **Vibration**: Choose whether the alarm uses vibration alert.

- **Snooze**: Allow snoozing. Set interval and repeat values for the alarm while snoozing.

3. Tap **Save** to save the alarm.

Delete an alarm

You can delete an alarm that you created.

1. From **Clock**, touch and hold an alarm.

2. Tap **Delete**.

World clock

The World clock lets you keep track of the current time in multiple cities around the globe.

1. From ⏰ **Clock**, tap **World clock**.

2. Tap ➕ **Add city** > **Search for a city**, and enter the name of the city.

3. Tap the city name in the list, and then tap Add.

   - To remove a city, touch and hold it, and tap 🗑 **Delete**.

Time zone converter

Set a time in a city on your World clock list to see what the local times would be in the other listed cities.

1. From ⏰ **Clock**, tap World clock.

2. Tap **More options** > **Time zone converter**.

3. Tap **Menu** to choose a different city.

   - To add a city to the list, tap **Add city**.

4. Swipe the hours, minutes, and period (**AM** or **PM**) on the clock to set a time. Local times for the other cities listed are automatically updated.

   - To return the clock to the current time, tap Reset.

Weather settings

Show weather information on your World clock.

1. From **Clock**, tap World clock.

2. Tap **More options** > **Settings** > **Show weather** to enable or disable weather information.

3. Tap Temperature to change from Fahrenheit to Celsius.

Stopwatch

The Stopwatch lets you time events down to a hundredth of a second.

1. From **Clock**, tap **Stopwatch.**

2. Tap **Start** to begin timing.

    - To keep track of lap times, tap **Lap**.

3. Tap **Stop** to end timing.

    - To continue timing after stopping the clock, tap **Resume.**

    - To reset the Stopwatch to zero, tap **Reset.**

Timer

Set a countdown timer for up to 99 hours, 59 minutes, and 59 seconds.

1. From ⊙ **Clock**, tap **Timer**.

2. Use the keypad and tap **Hours**, **Minutes**, and **Seconds** to set the Timer.

3. Tap **Start** to begin the Timer.

    - To temporarily stop the Timer, tap **Pause**. To continue, tap **Resume**.

    - To stop and reset the Timer, tap **Cancel**.

Preset timer

Name and save preset timers.

1. From ⊙ **Clock**, tap Timer > ＋ **Add preset timer.**

2. Configure the countdown time and timer name. Tap **Add** to save the timer.

   - To edit a saved preset timer, tap ⋮ **More options > Edit preset timers**.

Timer options

You can customize the Timer options.

1. From ◉ **Clock**, tap Timer.

2. Tap ⋮ **More options > Settings**.

   - **Sound**: Choose a preloaded timer sound or add your own.

   - **Vibration**: Enable to disable vibration for the timer.

General settings

View and configure settings for all Clock tools.

  o From ◉ Clock, tap ⋮ **More options > Settings**.

   - **Vibrate for alarms and timers**: Enable to always vibrate for alarms and timers if the Sound mode is set to either Mute or Vibrate.

- **Customization Service**: Sign in to your Samsung account to customize personal content in supported apps.

- **About Clock**: View the current software version and check for updates.

Contacts

Store and manage your contacts. You can synchronize with personal accounts added to your device. Accounts may also support email, calendars, and other features.

- From Apps, tap Contacts > Create contact.

Edit a contact

When editing a contact, you can tap a field and change or delete information, or you can add more fields to the contact's list of information.

1. From **Contacts**, tap a contact.
2. Tap **Edit**.
3. Tap any of the fields to add, change, or delete information.
4. Tap Save.

Call or message a contact

You can quickly call or message a contact using their default phone number.

1. From **Contacts**, tap a contact.
2. Tap **Call** or **Message.**

Favorites

When you mark contacts as favorites, they are easily accessible from other apps.

1. From **Contacts**, tap a contact.

2. Tap ☆ **Add to Favorites** to mark the contact as a favorite.

- To remove the contact from Favorites, tap ☆ **Favorite.**

Share a contact

Share a contact with others by using various sharing methods and services.

1. From **Contacts**, tap a contact.

2. Tap **Share**.

3. Tap either **File** or Text.

4. Choose a sharing method and follow the prompts.

Tip: When viewing a contact, tap **QR code** to quickly share the information with friends or family. The QR code automatically updates when you change the contact information fields.

Direct share

Share content directly with your contacts from within any app. Once enabled, your frequent contacts are displayed in the Share window.

- From Settings, tap **Advanced features** > **Direct share**, and tap to enable the feature.

Groups

You can use groups to organize your contacts.

Create a group

Create your own contact groups.

1. From **Contacts**, tap **Open drawer** > **Groups**.

2. Tap Create group, and then tap fields to enter information about the group:

• **Group name**: Enter a name for the new group.

• **Group ringtone**: Customize the sounds for the group.

• **Add member**: Select contacts to add to the new group, and then tap **Done**.

3. Tap Save.

Add or remove group contacts

Add more contacts to a group, or remove contacts.

- From **Contacts**, tap **Open drawer** > **Groups**, and then tap a group.

- To remove a contact, touch and hold a contact to select it, and then tap 🗑 **Remove**.

- To add a contact, tap ✏ **Edit** > **Add member**, and then tap the contacts you want to add. When finished, tap **Done** > **Save**.

Send a message to a group

Send a text message to members of a group.

1. From 👤 **Contacts**, tap ☰ **Open drawer** > **Groups**, and then tap a group.

2. Tap ⋮ **More options** > Send message.

Send an email to a group

Send an email to members of a group.

1. From 👤 **Contacts**, tap ☰ **Open drawer** > **Groups**, and then tap a group.

2. Tap ⋮ **More options** > **Send email**.

3. Tap contacts to select them, or tap the **All** checkbox at the top of the screen to select all, and then tap **Done**.

- Only group members that have an email address in their records are displayed.

4. Choose an email account and follow the prompts.

Delete a group

Delete a group you have created.

1. From **Contacts**, tap **Open drawer** > **Groups**, and then tap a group.

2. Tap **More options** > **Delete.**

    - To only delete the group, tap **Group only**.
    - To delete the group and the contacts in the group, tap **Group and members.**

Manage contacts

You can import or export contacts, as well as links multiple contacts into one contact entry.

Import contacts

Import contacts to your device as vCard files (VCF).

1. From **Contacts**, tap **Open drawer** > **manage contacts.**

2. Tap **Import or export contacts**.

3. Tap **Import** and follow the prompts.

Export contacts

Export contacts from your device as vCard files (VCF).

1. From **Contacts** tap **Open drawer** > **manage contacts**.
2. Tap **Import or export contacts.**
3. Tap **Export** and follow the prompts.

Link contacts

Consolidate contact information from multiple sources into one contact by linking entries into a single contact.

1. From **Contacts**, tap the contact to select it.
2. Tap **More options** > Link to another contact.
3. Tap contacts to choose them.
4. Tap Link.

To unlink contacts:

1. From **Contacts**, tap the contact to select it.
2. Tap **More options** > **Add/remove linked contacts.**

3. Tap **Unlink** beside contacts to unlink them from the main contact.

Delete contacts

Delete a single contact or multiple contacts.

1. From **Contacts**, touch and hold a contact to select it.

    - You can also tap other contacts to select them for deletion.

2. Tap **Delete**, and confirm when prompted.

Internet

Samsung Internet is a simple, fast, and reliable web browser for your device. Experience more secure Web browsing features with Secret Mode, Biometric Web Login, and Contents Blocker.

  o From Apps, tap Samsung folder > Internet.

Browser tabs

Use tabs to view multiple web pages at the same time.

○ From **Internet**, tap **Tabs** > New tab.

• To close a tab, tap **Tabs** > ✕ Close tab.

Bookmarks

The Bookmarks page stores Bookmarks, Saved pages, and your browsing History.

Open a Bookmark

Quickly launch a web page from the Bookmarks page.

1. From **Internet**, tap **Bookmarks.**

2. Tap a bookmark entry.

Save a web page

Saving a web page stores its content on your device so that you can access it offline.

- From **Internet**, tap **Tools** > **Add page to** > **Saved pages.**

Note: To view saved web pages, tap **Tools** > **Saved pages.**

View history

To view a list of recently visited web pages:

- From **Internet**, tap **Tools** > **History**.

TIP: To clear your browsing history, tap **More options** > **Clear history.**

Share pages

Web pages can be shared with your contacts.

- From **Internet**, tap **Tools** > **Share**, and follow the prompts.

Secret mode

Pages viewed in Secret mode are not listed in your browser history or search history, and leave no traces (such as cookies) on your device. Secret tabs are a darker shade than the normal tab windows.

Any downloaded files remain on your device after you close the secret tab.

1. From **Internet**, tap **Tabs** > **Turn on Secret mode**. Tap any of the following features for additional protection:

• Smart anti-tracking

• Ask sites not to track me

• Lock Secret mode

   3. Tap **Start** to begin browsing in Secret mode.

To turn off Secret mode:

   o From **Internet**, tap **Tabs** > **Turn off Secret mode.**

Internet settings

Modify settings associated with using the Internet app.

o From **Internet**, tap **Tools** > **Settings**.

💬 Messages

Keep in touch with your contacts by using the Messages app to share photos, send emojis, or just say a quick hello.

- From Apps, tap 💬 **Messages** > 📝 **Compose new message**.

Message Search

To quickly locate a message, use the search feature.

1. From 💬 **Messages**, tap 🔍 **Search**.
2. Enter keywords in the Search field, and then tap 🔍 **Search** on the keyboard.

Delete conversations

You can remove your conversion history by deleting conversations.

1. From **Messages**, tap **More options** > **Delete**.

2. Tap each conversation you want to delete.

3. Tap **Delete**, and confirm when prompted.

Emergency alerts

Emergency alerts notify you of imminent threats and other situations. There is no charge for receiving an Emergency alert message.

1. From **Messages**, tap **More options** > **Settings**.

2. Tap Emergency alert settings to customize notifications for emergency alerts.

Send SOS messages

Send a message with your location to designated contacts when you are in an emergency situation.

1. From Settings, tap **Advanced features** > **Send SOS messages**, and then tap to enable this feature.

2. Tap **Send messages** to and add recipients by creating new contacts or selecting from Contacts.

    - To include a picture from your front and rear camera, tap **Attach pictures**.

    - To include a five-second audio recording in your SOS message, tap **Attach audio recording**.

3. Press the **Side** key quickly three times to send an SOS message.

Message settings

Configure the settings for text and multimedia messages.

  o From **Messages**, tap **More options** > **Settings**.

My Files

View and manage files stored on your device, including images, videos, music, and sound clips.

- From Apps, tap Samsung folder >  **My Files**.

File groups

Files stored in the device are organized into the following groups:

- **Recent files**: View recently accessed files.
- **Categories**: View your files based on the file type.
- **Storage**: View files saved on your device and cloud accounts.

— Cloud drives vary depending on the services you sign in to.

• **Analyze storage**: See what's taking up space in your storage.

My Files options

Use My Files options to search, edit, clear file history, and more.

- From **My Files**, the following options are available:

- Search: Search for a file or folder.

- **More options**:

  - **Clear Recent files list**: Remove the list of recently accessed files. This option is only available after a file has been opened through My Files.

  - **Analyze storage**: See what's taking up space in your storage.

  - **Trash**: Choose to restore or permanently remove files that you delete.

  - **Settings**: View settings for the app.

Phone

The Phone app does more than just make telephone calls. Explore the advanced calling features.

○ From a Home screen, tap **Phone.**

Calls

The Phone app allows you to make and answer calls from the Home screen, Recent tab, contact and more.

Make a call

Use your phone to make and answer calls from a Home screen.

- From **Phone**, enter a number on the keypad and tap **Call**.
  - Tap Keypad if the keypad is not displayed.

Enable swipe to call

Swipe a contact or number to the right to make a call.

1. From Settings, tap **Advanced features** > Motions and gestures > **Swipe to call or send messages.**

2. Tap to enable this feature.

Make a call from Recent

All incoming, outgoing, and missed calls are recorded in the Call log.

1. From **Phone**, tap **Recents** to display a list of recent calls.

2. Tap a contact, and then tap Call.

Make a call from Contacts

Call a contact from the Contacts app.

- From **Contacts**, swipe your finger across a contact to the right to call the contact.

Answer a call

When a call is received, the phone rings and the caller's phone number or name is displayed. If you are using an app, a pop-up screen is displayed for the incoming call.

- On the incoming call screen, drag **Answer** to the right to answer the call.

Tip: On the incoming call pop-up screen, tap **Answer** to answer the call.

Decline a call

You can choose to decline an incoming call. If you are using an app, a pop-up screen is displayed for the incoming call.

- On the incoming call screen, drag **Decline** to the left to reject the call and send it to your voicemail.

TIP: On the incoming pop-up screen, tap **Decline** to reject the call and send it to your voicemail.

Decline with a message

You can choose to decline an incoming call with a text message response.

- On the incoming call screen, drag **Send message** upward and select a message.

Tip: On the incoming call pop-up screen, tap **Send message** and select a message.

End a call

- Tap ⌒ End when you are ready to end your call.

Actions while on a call

You can adjust call volume, switch to a headset or speaker, and even multitask while on a call.

- Press the **Volume** keys to increase or decrease the volume.

Switch to headset or speaker

Listen to the call using the speaker or through a Bluetooth® headset (not included).

- Tap 🔊 **Speaker** to hear the caller using the speaker or tap 🔷 **Bluetooth** to hear the caller using a Bluetooth headset.

Multitask

If you exit the call screen to use another app, your active call is indicated in the Status bar.

To return to the call screen:

- Drag the Status bar down to display the Notification panel and tap the call.

To end a call while multitasking:

- Drag the Status bar down to display the Notification panel, and then tap End 📞 **call**.

Call pop-up settings

When calls are received while using other apps, they can be displayed as pop-ups.

- From 📞 **Phone**, tap ⋮ **More options** > **Settings** > **Call display while using apps**. The following options are available:
    - **Full screen**: Display an incoming call in the full screen Phone app.

- **Pop-up**: Display an incoming call as a pop-up at the top of the screen.

- **Mini pop-up**: Display an incoming call as a smaller pop-up.

- **Keep calls in pop-up**: Enable this option to keep calls in the pop-up after they are answered.

Places

Explore nearby business and venues to get contact information and directions.

1. From ▇ **Phone**, tap **Places**.
2. Tap a category to search nearby.
3. Tap a location to view contact information and directions.

Note: Location services must be enabled to use this feature.

Manage calls

Your calls are recorded in a call log. You can set up speed dials, block numbers, and use voicemail.

Call log

The numbers of the calls you have dialed, received, or missed are stored in the Call log.

- From **Phone**, tap **Recent**. A list of recent calls is displayed. If the caller is in your Contacts list, the caller's name is displayed.

Save a contact from a recent call

Use recent call information to create a contact or update your Contacts list.

1. From **Phone, tap Recent**.
2. Tap the call that contains the information that you want to save to your Contacts list, and **tap Add to contacts.**
3. Tap Create new contact or Update existing contact.

Delete call records

To delete Call log entries:

1. From P **phone**, tap **Recent**.
2. Touch and hold the call you want to delete from the Call log.
3. Tap **Delete**.

Block a number

By adding a caller to your Block list, future calls from this number are sent directly to your voicemail, and messages are not received.

1. From **Phone**, tap **Recents**.

2. Tap the caller you want to add to the Block list.

3. Tap **Details** > **Block**, and confirm when prompted.

TIP: You can also modify your Block list in Settings. From **Phone**, tap **More options** > **Settings** > **Block numbers.**

Speed dial

You can assign a shortcut number to a contact for speed dialing their default number.

1. From **Phone, tap Keypad** > **More options** > **Speed dial numbers**. The Speed dial numbers screen displays the reserved speed dial numbers.

2. Tap an unassigned number.

- Tap ▼ **Menu** to select a different Speed dial number than the next one in sequence.

- Number 1 is reserved for Voicemail.

3. Type in a name or number, or tap **Add from Contacts** to assign a contact to the number.

- The selected contact is displayed in the Speed dial number box.

Make a call with Speed dial

You can make a call using Speed dial.

o From **Phone**, touch and hold the Speed dial number.

- If the Speed dial number is more than one digit long, enter the first digits, and then hold the last digit.

Remove a Speed dial number

1. You can remove an assigned Speed dial number. From **Phone**, tap ⋮ **More options** > **Speed dial numbers.**

2. Tap **Delete** by the contact you want to remove from Speed dial.

Voicemail

Use your phone's voicemail feature.

1. From **Phone**, touch and hold the **1 key**.
2. Follow the voice prompts from the voicemail center

Emergency calls

You can dial the emergency telephone number in your region regardless of the phone's service status. If your phone is not activated, you can only make an emergency call.

1. From **Phone**, enter the emergency telephone number (911 in North America) and **tap Call.**
2. Complete your call. During this type of call, you have access to most in-call features.

TIP: The emergency telephone number can be dialed even if the phone is locked, allowing anyone to use your phone to call for help in an emergency. When accessed from a locked screen, only the emergency calling feature is accessible to the caller. The rest of the phone remains secured.

Phone settings

These settings allow you to modify settings associated with the Phone app.

- From **Phone, tap** **More options** > Settings.

Optional calling services

If available with your service plan, the following calling services are supported.

Place a multi-party call

If your service plan supports this feature, you can make another call while a call is in progress.

1. From the active call, tap **Add call** to dial the second call.

2. Dial the new number and tap **Call**. When the call is answered:

    - Tap **Swap** to switch between the two calls.
    - Tap **Merge** to hear both callers at once (multi-conferencing).

TTY mode

A teletypewriter (TTY) is a telecommunications device that allows people who are deaf, hard of hearing, or who have speech or language disabilities to communicate by telephone.

1. From Phone, tap More options > Settings.

2. Tap **Other call settings** > **TTY mode**.

3. Tap TTY Off, TTY Full, TTY HCO, or TTY VCO.

Samsung Health

Use Samsung Health™ to plan, track various aspects of daily life contributing to well-being such as physical activity, diet, and sleep.

From Apps, tap Samsung folder > Samsung Health.

Note: The information gathered from this device, Samsung Health, or related software is not intended for use in the diagnosis of disease or other conditions, or in the cure, mitigation, treatment or prevention of disease.

The accuracy of the information and data provided by this device and its related software, may be affected by factors such as environmental conditions, specific activity performed while using/wearing the device, settings of the device, user configuration/user-provided information, and other end-user interactions.

Before you start exercising

Although the Samsung Health application is a great companion to your exercise routine, it is always best to make sure you consult with your physician before beginning any exercise regimen. While moderate physical activity, such as brisk walking, is safe for most people, health experts suggest that you talk with your doctor before you start an exercise program, particularly if you have any of the following conditions:

- Heart disease; Asthma or lung disease; Diabetes, or liver or kidney disease; and Arthritis

Before beginning your exercise regimen check with your doctor if you have symptoms suggestive of heart, lung, or other serious disease, such as:

- Pain or discomfort in your chest, neck, jaw, or arms during physical activity;
- Dizziness or loss of consciousness;

- Shortness of breath with mild exertion or at rest, or when lying down or going to bed;

- Ankle swelling, especially at night;

- heart murmur or a rapid or pronounced heartbeat;

- Muscle pain when walking upstairs or up a hill that goes away when you rest.

It is recommended that before engaging in an exercise routine, you consult with your doctor or medical practitioner. If you are unsure of your health status, have several health problems, or are pregnant, you should speak with your doctor before starting a new exercise program.

Samsung Notes

Use Samsung Notes to create notes containing text, images with footnotes, voice recordings, and music. You can share your notes easily using social networking services.

○ From Apps, tap Samsung Notes > Create.

Create notes

Add text, images, voice recordings and more.

1. From **Samsung Notes**, tap **Create note**.

2. When you are finished, tap **Save**.

Edit notes

Make edits to notes you create.

- From **Samsung Notes**, tap a note to view it.

- Tap Edit and make changes. When you are finished, tap **Save**.

Notes options

You can edit, sort, or manage notes.

- From 🗎 Samsung Notes, tap ⋮ More options for the following options:
    - **Edit**: Select notes to share, delete, lock, or move.
    - **Sort**: Change the way notes are organized.
    - **View**: Switch between Grid, List, or Simple list.

Notes menu

You can view your notes by category.

- From 🗎 Samsung Notes, tap ☰ **Navigation drawer** for the following options:
    - **All notes**: View all notes.
    - **Frequently used**: Quick access to commonly used notes.
    - **Shared notebooks**: View notebooks shared with your contacts through your Samsung account.

- **Trash**: View deleted notes for up to 15 days.

- **Categories**: View notes by category.

- **Settings**: View settings for the Samsung Notes app.

- **Manage categories**: Add, remove, and organize categories.

Samsung Pay

Samsung Pay™ lets you make payments with your device. It is accepted almost anywhere you can swipe or tap your credit card. A Samsung account is required.

- From Apps, tap **Samsung Pay**, and tap Get started and follow the prompts.

Note: For added security, your credit and debit card information is not stored on a cloud service. If you are using the Samsung Pay app on multiple devices, you must sign in to the app and confirm all payment cards on each device.

Some card issuers may limit the number of devices. Use Samsung Pay

Use Samsung Pay

By opening the app and holding your device over the stores card reader.

1. From Apps, tap **Samsung Pay**, select a card to pay with and authorize payments by scanning your finger or by entering your Samsung Pay PIN.

2. Hold your phone over the store's card reader.

   - When your payment is complete, a receipt is sent to your registered email.

Note: Make sure the NFC feature is enabled on your device.

Simple Pay

Use Simply Pay to access Samsung Pay from the Lock Screen, Home screen, or Always On Display.

1. From Apps, tap **Samsung Pay**, tap **Menu** > **Settings** > **Use Favorite Cards**.

2. Tap to enable Simple Pay on each screen.

To use Simple Pay:

1. From any screen, swipe up from the bottom of the screen.

- Your payment card and Simple Pay are displayed.

2. Drag the card down to close Simple Pay.

Use gift cards with Samsung Pay

Purchase, send, and redeem gift cards from an expanding selection of your favorite retailers.

Secure your information

Samsung Pay is designed with the latest security technology and works on most recent Samsung Galaxy devices. Payments are authorized with your fingerprint or PIN, and each transaction uses a unique token each time, so your device only allows payments with your consent.

If your device is ever lost, you can use the Find My Mobile function to remotely wipe your data for even more protection.

Google apps:

Enjoy these apps from Google

 **Chrome**

Browse the Internet with Chrome™ and bring your open tabs, bookmarks, and address bar data from your computer to your mobile device.

 Drive

Open, view, rename, and share files saved to your Google Drive™ cloud account.

 Duo

Make one-to-one video calls.

 Gmail

Send and receive email with Google's web-based email service.

 Google

Find online content with tools that learn what interests you. Turn on your personalized feed to receive customized content.

 Maps

Get directions and other location-based information. You must enable location services to use Google Maps.

 Photos

Store and back up your photos and videos automatically to your Google Account with Google Photos™.

 Play Movies & TV

Watch movies and TV shows purchased from Google Play. You can also view videos saved on your device.

 Play Store

Find new apps, movies and TV shows, music, books, magazines, and games in the Google Play store.

 YouTube

Watch and upload YouTube™ videos right from your device.

 YT Music

Stream and browse playlists, albums, and artists from YouTube Music.

Microsoft apps:

Enjoy these apps from Microsoft.

 **Outlook**

Access email, calendar, contacts, tasks, and more in Outlook. See **Add an Outlook account.**

- From Apps, tap **Microsoft folder > Outlook.**

LinkedIn

Connect and network with other professionals around the world.

 **OneDrive**

Store and share photos, videos, documents, and more in your free online OneDrive® account—accessible from your personal computer, tablet, or phone.

Additional apps

The following apps are preloaded or downloaded over-the-air to your device.

 Facebook

Keep up with friends and family with the Facebook™ app. Share updates, photos, and videos, as well as text, chat, and play games.

 Netflix

Stream movies and TV shows on your device using your Netflix.com account.

 **Spotify**

Access music and podcasts on your device. You can listen to artists and albums, or create your own playlist of your favorite songs.

Chapter 5
Settings

Access Settings

There are a couple of ways to access your device settings.

- Drag down the Status bar, and then tap ⚙ **Settings.**

- From Apps, tap ⚙ **Settings.**

Search for Settings

If you are not sure exactly where to find a certain setting, you can search for it.

1. From Settings, tap 🔍 **Search**, and enter keywords.

2. Tap an entry to go to that setting.

Connections:

Manage connections between your device and a variety of networks and other devices.

Wi-Fi

You can connect your device to a Wi-Fi network to access the Internet without using your mobile data.

1. From Settings, tap 📶 **Connections > Wi-Fi**, and then ⬤ tap to turn on Wi-Fi and scan for available networks.

2. Tap a network, and enter a password if required.

Manually connect to a Wi-Fi network

If the Wi-Fi network you want is not listed after a scan, you can still connect to it by entering the information manually.

Ask the Wi-Fi network administrator for the name and password before you begin.

1. From Settings, tap **Connections** > **Wi-Fi**, and then tap to turn on Wi-Fi.

2. Tap **Add network** at the bottom of the list.

3. Enter information about the Wi-Fi network:

    Network name: Type the exact name of the network.

    - **Security**: Select a security option from the list, and enter the password if required.

    - **MAC address type**: Choose which type of MAC address to use for this connection.

    - **Auto reconnects**: Choose this option if you want to automatically reconnect to this network whenever you are in range.

- **Advanced**: Add any advanced options, such as IP and Proxy settings.

4. Tap **Save**.

Tip: Tap ▦ to connect to a Wi-Fi network by using your device's camera to scan a QR code.

Advanced Wi-Fi settings

You can configure connections to various types of Wi-Fi networks and hotspots, manage saved networks and look up your device's network addresses.

1. From Settings, tap 📶 **Connections** > **Wi-Fi**, and then tap t ⬤ to turn on Wi-Fi.

2. Tap ⋮ **More options** > **Advanced**.

    - **Switch to mobile data**: When enabled, your device will switch to mobile data whenever the Wi-Fi connection is unstable. When the Wi-Fi signal is strong, it switches back to Wi-Fi.

    - **Turn on Wi-Fi automatically**: Turn on Wi-Fi in frequently-used locations.

- **Network notification**: Receive notifications when open networks in range are detected.

- **Manage networks**: View saved Wi-Fi networks and configure whether to auto reconnect to or forget individual networks.

- **Wi-Fi control history**: View apps that have recently turned your Wi-Fi on or off.

- **Hotspot 2.0**: Connect automatically to Wi-Fi networks that support Hotspot 2.0.

- **Install network certificates**: Install authentication certificates.

- **MAC address**: View your device's MAC address, which is required when connecting to some secured networks (not configurable).

- **IP address**: View your device's IP address (not configurable).

Wi-Fi Direct

Uses Wi-Fi to share data between devices.

1. From Settings, tap **Connections** > Wi-Fi, and then tap to turn on Wi-Fi.

2. Tap **More options** > **Wi-Fi Direct**.

3. Tap a device, and then follow the prompts to connect.

Tip: When sharing a file, tap Wi-Fi Direct to use this feature.

Disconnect from Wi-Fi Direct

Disconnect your device from a Wi-Fi Direct device.

- From Settings, tap **Connections** > **Wi-Fi** > **Wi-Fi Direct**. Tap a device to disconnect it

Bluetooth

You can pair your device to other Bluetooth-enabled devices, like Bluetooth headphones or a Bluetooth-enabled vehicle infotainment system. Once a pairing is created, the devices remember each other and can exchange information without having to enter the passkey again.

1. From Settings, tap 🛜 Connections > **Bluetooth**, and then tap ⬤ to turn on Bluetooth.

2. Tap a device and follow the prompts to connect.

Tip: When sharing a file, tap 🔵 **Bluetooth** to use this feature.

Rename a paired device

You can rename a paired device to make it easier to recognize.

1. From Settings, tap 🛜 **Connections** > **Bluetooth**, and then tap ⬤ to turn on Bluetooth.

2. Tap ⚙ **Settings** next to the device name and then tap **Rename**.

3. Enter a new name, and tap **Rename**.

Unpair from a Bluetooth device

When you unpair from a Bluetooth device, the two devices no longer recognize each other.

1. From Settings, tap **Connections** > **Bluetooth**, and then tap to turn on Bluetooth.

2. Tap **Settings** next to the device, and then tap **Unpair**.

Tip: You will need to pair with the device again in order to connect to it.

Advanced options

Additional Bluetooth features are available in the advanced menu.

1. From Settings, tap **Connections** > **Bluetooth**.

2. Tap Advanced for the following options:

    - **Music Share**: Let friends play music on your Bluetooth speaker or headphones.

    - **Ringtone sync**: Use the ringtone set on your phone when you receive calls through a connected Bluetooth device.

    - **Bluetooth control history**: View apps that have used Bluetooth recently.

Dual audio

1. You can play audio from your device to two connected Bluetooth audio devices.

2. Connect Bluetooth audio devices to your Smartphone.

3. From the Notification panel, tap **Media**.

4. Under Audio output, tap next to each audio device to play audio to them (up to two devices).

NFC and payment

Near Field Communication (NFC) allows you to communicate with another device without connecting to a network. This technology is used by Android Beam and certain payment apps. The device that you are transferring to needs to support NFC, and it needs to be within four centimeters of your device.

- From Settings, tap **Connections > NFC and payment**, and then tap to turn on this feature.

Android Beam

Use Android Beam to share photos, contacts, or other data between NFC-enabled devices.

1. From Settings, tap 🛜 **Connections** > **NFC and payment**, and then tap ⚪ to turn on NFC.

2. Tap Android Beam, and then tap to turn on this feature.

Tip: When sharing a file, tap 🔵 **Android Beam** to use this feature.

Tap and pay

Use an NFC payment app to make payments by touching your device to a compatible credit card reader.

1. From Settings, tap 🛜 **Connections** > **NFC and payment**, and then tap ⚪ to turn on NFC.

2. Tap and pay > Payment to see the default payment app.

    - To use another payment app when it is open instead of the default app, tap **and pay with open apps.**

    - To set another payment app as the default, tap **Others,** and then tap the app you prefer.

Airplane mode

Airplane mode disconnects your device from all networks and turns off connectivity features.

1. From Settings, tap 🛜 **Connections** > **Airplane mode.**

2. Tap ⬤ to enable this feature.

Mobile networks

Use Mobile networks to configure your device's ability to connect to mobile networks and use mobile data.

- From Settings, tap 🛜 **Connections** > **Mobile networks**.

    - **Data roaming**: Enable data usage while roaming on other mobile networks.

    - **Network mode**: You can select which network modes your mobile device can use.

    - **Access Point Names**: Choose or add APNs, which have the network settings your device needs to connect to your provider.

    - **Network operators**: Choose available and preferred networks.

Tip: Use these features to help manage connection settings that may affect your monthly bill.

Data usage

Check your current mobile and Wi-Fi data usage. You can also customize warnings and limits.

- From Settings, tap 🛜 **Connections > Data usage.**

Turn on Data saver

Use Data saver to reduce your data consumption by preventing selected apps from sending or receiving data in the background.

1. From Settings, tap 🛜 **Connections > Data usage > Data saver**.

2. Tap ⬤ to turn on Data saver.

    - To allow some apps to have unrestricted data usage, tap **Allow app while Data saver on**, and tap ⬤ next to each app to specify restrictions.

Monitor mobile data

You can customize your mobile data access by setting limits and restrictions.

- From Settings, tap 🛜 **Connections** > **Data usage**. The following options are available:

    - **Mobile data**: Use mobile data from your plan.

    - **Mobile data only apps**: Set apps to always use mobile data, even when your device is connected to Wi-Fi.

    - **Mobile data usage**: View data usage over mobile connections over a period of time. You can view total usage as well as usage by app.

    - **Billing cycle and data warning**: Change the monthly date to align with your carrier's billing date.

Tip: Use these features to keep an eye on your estimated data usage.

Monitor Wi-Fi data

You can restrict Wi-Fi data access by customizing usage limits and networks.

1. From Settings, tap 🛜 **Connections** > **Data usage.**

2. Tap **Wi-Fi data usage** to view data usage over Wi-Fi connections over a period of time. You can view total usage as well as usage by app.

Mobile hotspot

Mobile hotspot uses your data plan to create a Wi-Fi network that can be used by multiple devices.

1. From Settings, tap 🛜 **Connections** > **Mobile hotspot and tethering** > **Mobile hotspot**.

2. Tap ⬤ to turn on Mobile hotspot.

3. On the devices you want to connect, activate Wi-Fi and select your device's Mobile hotspot. Enter the Mobile hotspot password to connect.

   - To view a list of devices that are connected to your Mobile hotspot, tap **connected devices**.

Change the Mobile hotspot password

You can customize your Mobile hotspot password to make it easier to remember.

1. From Settings, tap 🛜 **Connections** > **Mobile hotspot and tethering** > **Mobile hotspot**.

2. Tap the password, enter a new password, and then tap **Save**.

Configure mobile hotspot settings

You can customize your mobile hotspot's security and connection settings.

1. From Settings, tap 🛜 **Connections** > **Mobile hotspot and tethering** > **Mobile hotspot**.

2. Tap ⋮ **More options** > **Configure mobile hotspot** for the following settings:

    - **Network name**: View and change the name of your Mobile hotspot.

    - **Hide my device**: Prevent your Mobile hotspot from being discoverable by other devices.

- **Security**: Choose the security level for your Mobile hotspot.

- **Password**: If you choose a security level that uses a password, you can view or change it.

- **Protected management frames**: Enable this feature for additional privacy protections.

Timeout settings

You can set the Mobile hotspot to automatically turn off when there are no connected devices.

1. From Settings, tap 🛜 **Connections** > **Mobile hotspot and tethering** > **Mobile hotspot**.

2. Tap ⋮ **More options** > **Timeout settings**, and then select an interval.

Tip: This feature can help you manage your data usage

Wi-Fi sharing

Turn on Wi-Fi sharing to quickly share your Wi-Fi network with other devices.

1. From Settings, tap 🛜 **Connections** > **Mobile hotspot and tethering** > **Mobile hotspot**.

2. Tap **More options** > **Wi-Fi sharing** to turn on this feature.

Tip: Use this feature to share your Wi-Fi network without giving out your Wi-Fi password.

Band

Select one of the available bandwidth options.

1. From Settings, tap **Connections** > **Mobile hotspot and tethering** > **Mobile hotspot**.

2. Tap **Band**, and tap an option.

Auto hotspot

Share your hotspot connection with other devices signed in to your Samsung account.

1. From Settings, tap **Connections** > **Mobile hotspot and tethering** > **Mobile hotspot**.

2. Tap Auto hotspot, and tap to enable the feature.

Tethering

You can use tethering to share your device's Internet connection with another device.

1. From Settings, tap 📶 **Connections** > **Mobile hotspot and tethering.**

2. Tap an option:

    - Tap **Bluetooth tethering** to share your device's Internet connection using Bluetooth.

    - Connect the computer to the device using a USB cable, and then tap **USB tethering**.

Nearby device scanning

Easily set up connections to other available devices by turning on Nearby device scanning. This feature sends you a notification when there are available devices to connect to.

1. From Settings, tap 📶 **Connections** > **More connection settings** >**Nearby device scanning**.

2. Tap to turn on the feature.

Connect to a printer

Connect your device to a printer on the same Wi-Fi network to easily print documents and images from your device.

1. From Settings, tap 🛜 **Connections** > **More connection settings** > **Printing**.

2. Tap ➕ **Download plugin** and follow the prompts to add a print service.

3. Tap the print service, and then tap ⋮ **More options** > **Add printer**.

Note: Not all apps support printing.

MirrorLink

If your car is compatible with MirrorLink™ you can mirror your device's display on your car's entertainment and information screen using a USB connection.

1. Connect your device to your car's system using the USB cable.

2. From Settings, tap 🛜 **Connections** > **More connection settings** > **MirrorLink**.

3. Tap **Connect to car via USB**, and follow the prompts.

Virtual Private Networks

A Virtual Private Network (VPN) allows you to connect to a private secured network from your device. You will need the connection information from your VPN administrator.

1. From Settings, tap **Connections** > **More connection settings** > **VPN**.

2. Tap **More options** > **Add VPN profile**.

3. Enter the VPN network information provided by your network administrator, and tap **Save**.

Tip: A secured screen lock is required to set up a VPN.

Manage a VPN

Use the VPN settings menu to edit or delete a VPN connection.

1. From Settings, tap **Connections** > **More connection settings** > **VPN**.

2. Tap Settings next to a VPN.

3. Edit the VPN and tap **Save**, or tap **Delete** to remove the VPN.

Connect to a VPN

Once you have set up a VPN, connecting to and disconnecting from a VPN is easy.

1. From Settings, tap **Connections** > **More connection settings** > **VPN**.

2. Tap a **VPN**, enter your log in information, and tap **Connect**.

   - To disconnect, tap the VPN, and then tap **Disconnect**.

Private DNS

You can configure your device to connect to a private DNS host.

1. From Settings, tap **Connections** > **More connection settings** > **Private DNS**.

2. Tap one of the available options to configure a private DNS connection.

3. Tap Save

Ethernet

If wireless network connection is not available, you can use an Ethernet cable to connect your device to a local network.

1. Connect an Ethernet cable to your device.

2. From Settings, tap 📶 **Connections** > **More connection settings** > **Ethernet, and follow the** prompts.

Tip: You need an adapter (not included) to connect an Ethernet cable to your device.

Chapter 6

Customization, Security, Accounts & Backup

Sounds and vibration

You can control the sounds and vibrations used to indicate notifications, screen touches, and other interactions.

Sound mode

You can change the sound mode on your device without using the volume keys.

- From Settings, tap **Sounds and vibration**, and then choose a mode:
  - **Sound**: Use the sounds, vibrations, and volume levels you have chosen in Sound settings for notifications and alerts.
  - **Vibrate while ringing**: Set your device to vibrate in addition to ringing when you receive a call.
  - **Vibrate**: Use vibration only for notifications and alerts.
  - **Mute**: Set your device to make no sounds.

- **Temporary mute**: Set a time limit for muting the device.

Tip: Use the sound mode setting instead of the volume keys to change the sound mode without losing your customized sound levels.

Easy mute

Quickly mute sounds by covering the screen or turning the device over.

- From Settings, tap **Advanced features** > **Motions and gestures** > **Easy mute**, and tap to enable.

Vibrations

You can control how and when your device vibrates

1. From Settings, tap **Sounds and vibration**.
2. Tap options to customize:
    - **Vibration pattern**: Choose from preset vibration patterns.

- **Vibration intensity**: Set vibration intensity levels for calls, notifications, and touch interactions by dragging the sliders.

Volume

Set the volume level for call ringtones, notifications, and other audio.

- From Settings, tap 🔊 **Sounds and vibration** > **Volume, and drag the sliders.**

Tip: You can also use the **Volume** key to adjust the volume. Slide the volume controls to customize all volume options.

Use Volume keys for media

Set the default of the Volume key to control the media volume.

1. From Settings, tap 🔊 **Sounds and vibration** > **Volume.**
2. Tap **Use Volume keys for media** to enable this feature.

Media volume limit

Limit the maximum output of the device's volume while using headphones or Bluetooth speakers (not included).

1. From Settings, tap **Sounds** and **vibration** > **Volume**.

2. Tap More options > Media volume limit.

3. Tap to enable this feature.

   - To set the maximum output volume, drag the **Custom volume limit** slider.

   - To require a PIN to make changes to the volume setting, tap Set volume **limit PIN.**

Ringtone

Customize your call ringtone by choosing from preset sounds or adding your own.

1. From Settings, tap **Sounds and vibration** > **Ringtone**.

2. Tap a ringtone to hear a preview and select it, or tap **Add** to use an audio file as a ringtone.

Notification sound

Choose a preset sound for all notification alerts.

1. From Settings, tap 🔊 **Sounds and vibration** > **Notification sound**.

2. Tap a sound to hear a preview and select it.

Tip: You can also customize notifications sounds to be unique for each app using the App settings menu.

System sound

Choose a sound theme to use for touch interactions, charging, changing the sound mode, and Samsung Keyboard.

- From Settings, tap 🔊 **Sounds and vibration** > **System sound** and choose an available option.

System sounds and vibration

Customize your device's sounds and vibrations for actions like tapping the screen and charging the device.

- From Settings, tap 🔊 **Sounds and vibration** > **System sound/vibration control** for the following options: **System sounds**
    - **Touch interactions**: Play tones when you touch or tap the screen to make selections.

- **Screen lock/unlock**: Play a sound when you lock or unlock the screen.

- **Charging**: Play a sound when a charger is connected.

- **Dialing keypad**: Play a tone when dialing numbers on the Phone keypad.

- **Samsung keyboard**: Play a sound when typing with the Samsung keyboard.

System vibration

- **Touch interactions**: Vibrate when you tap navigation buttons or touch and hold items on the screen.

- **Samsung keyboard**: Vibrate when typing with the Samsung keyboard.

Dolby Atmos

Enjoy Dolby Atmos quality when playing content that was specifically mixed for Atmos. This feature may only be available with a headset connected.

1. From Settings, tap 🔊 **Sounds and vibration** > **Sound quality and effects**.

2. Tap **Dolby Atmos** to experience breakthrough audio that flows above and around you.

Equalizer

Choose an audio preset that is customized to different genres of music, or manually change your audio settings.

1. From Settings, tap **Sounds and vibration** > **Sound quality and effects**.

2. Tap **Equalizer** to choose a music genre.

Headset audio options

Enhance the sound resolution of music and videos for a clearer listening experience. These features are only available with a headset connected.

- From Settings, tap **Sounds and vibration** > **Sound quality and effects**, and tap an option to turn it on:
    - **UHQ upscaler**: Sharpens audio resolution for crisp sound.

Adapt sound

Customize the sound for each ear and enhance your listening experience.

1. From Settings, tap 🔊 **Sounds and vibration** > **Sound quality and effects** > **Adapt sound.**

2. Tap the sound profile that fits your best, and tap ⚙**Settings** to customize.

Tip: Tap ➕ **Add personalized sound profile** to take a hearing test and let your device identify the best sound for you.

Separate app sound

You can play media sound on a speaker or headphones separate from the rest of the sounds on your device. Connect to a Bluetooth device to make this option available in the Audio device menu.

1. From Settings, tap 🔊 Sounds and vibration > Separate app sound.

2. Tap **Turn on now** to enable Separate app sound, and then set the following options:

    - **App**: Choose an app to play its sound on a separate audio device.

    - **Audio device**: Choose the audio device that you want the app's sound to be played on.

Notifications

You can prioritize and streamline app alerts by changing which apps send notifications and how notifications alert you.

Manage notifications

You can configure notifications from apps and services.

- From Settings, tap **Notifications**.

    - **Suggest actions and replies**: Get applicable suggestions for actions to notifications and replies to messages.

    - **Show snooze option**: Get an option to snooze a notification for a later time.

    - **App icon badges**: Identify which apps have active notifications with badges that appear on their icons. Tap to choose whether or not badges indicate the number of unread notifications.

    - **Status bar**: Modify how many notifications appear on the Status bar.

- **Do not disturb**: Block sounds and notifications while this mode is turned on. Specify exceptions for people, apps, and alarms.

- To block notifications from an app, tap next to the app. Tap **See all** to open the complete list of apps.

Customize app notifications

You can change notification settings for each app.

1. From Settings, tap **Notifications** >**See all**.

2. Tap an app for the following options:

- **Show notifications**: Receive notifications from this app.

- **Categories**: Configure notification options that are specific to this app.

- **App icon badges**: Show a badge on the icon when there are notifications.

Smart alert

You can set the device to notify you about missed calls and messages by vibrating when you pick it up.

- From Settings, tap **Advanced features** > **Motions and gestures** > **Smart alert**, and tap to enable.

Smart pop-up view

Receive notifications as icons that can be tapped and expanded in pop-up view.

- From Settings, tap **Advanced features** > **Smart pop-up** view, and tap to enable.

Display

You can configure the screen brightness, timeout delay, font size, and many other display settings.

Dark mode

Dark mode allows you to switch to a darker theme to keep your eyes more comfortable at night, darkening white or bright screens and notifications.

- From Settings, tap **Display**, and select one of the following options:
    - **Light**: Apply a light color theme to your device (Default).

- **Dark**: Apply a dark color theme to your device.

- **Dark mode settings**: Customize when and where Dark mode is applied.

    - **Turn on as scheduled**: Configure Dark mode for either Sunset to sunrise or Custom schedule

    - **Apply to wallpaper**: Apply Dark mode settings to the wallpaper when it is active.

    - **Adaptive color filter**: Turn on Blue light filter automatically between sunset and sunrise to reduce eye strain.

Screen brightness

Adjust the screen brightness according to lighting conditions or personal preference.

1. From Settings, tap **Display**.

2. Customize options under Brightness:

    - Drag the **Brightness** sliders to set a custom brightness level.

- Tap **Adaptive brightness** to automatically adjust the screen brightness based on the lighting conditions.

Blue light filter

The Blue light filter can help you sleep better if you use your device at night. You can set a schedule to automatically turn this feature on and off.

- From Settings, tap **Display>Blue light filter**, and then choose one of the following options:
    - Drag the Opacity slider to set the opacity of the filter.
    - Tap Turn on now to enable this feature.
    - Tap Turn on as scheduled to set a schedule for when Blue light filter should be enabled. You can choose Sunset to sunrise or Custom schedule.

Screen mode

Your device has several screen mode options which adjust the screen quality for different situations. You can select the mode according to your preference.

1. From Settings, tap ☀ **Display** > **Screen mode**.

2. Tap an option to set a different screen mode.

Font size and style

You can change the font size and style to customize your device.

- o From Settings, tap ☀ **Display** > **Font size and style** for the following options:
    - Tap **Font style** to choose a different font.
        - Tap a font to select it, or tap ➕ **Download fonts** to add fonts from Galaxy Store.
    - Tap **Bold font** to make all fonts appear with bold weight.
    - Drag the **Font size** slider to adjust the size of text.

Screen zoom

Adjust the zoom level to increase or decrease the size of content on the screen.

1. From Settings, tap ☀ **Display** > **Screen zoom**.

2. Drag the **Screen zoom** slider to adjust the zoom level.

Full screen apps

You can choose which apps you want to use in the full screen aspect ratio.

- From Settings, tap **Display** > **Full screen apps** and tap apps to enable this feature.

Screen timeout

You can set the screen to turn off after a set amount of time.

- From Settings, tap **Display** > Screen timeout, and tap a time limit to set it.

Note: Prolonged display of non-moving images, excluding Always On Display, may result in permanent ghost-like afterimages or degraded image quality. Turn off the display screen when not in use.

Accidental touch protection

Prevent the screen from detecting touch input while the device is in a dark place, such as a pocket or a bag.

- From Settings, tap **Display** > **Accidental touch protection** to enable or disable the feature.

Touch sensitivity

Increase the touch sensitivity of the screen for use with screen protectors.

- From Settings, tap **Display** > **Touch sensitivity** to enable

Show charging information

Battery level and estimated time until the device is fully charged can be displayed when the screen is off.

- From Settings, tap **Display** >**Show charging information** to enable.

Screen saver

You can display colors or photos when the screen turns off or while charging.

1. From Settings, tap **Display** > **Screen saver**.
2. Choose one of the following options:

- **None**: Do not display a screen saver.

- **Colors**: Tap the selector to display a changing screen of colors.

- **Photo table**: Display pictures in a photo table.

- **Photo frame**: Display pictures in a photo frame.

- **Photos**: Display pictures from your Google Photos account.

3. Tap **Preview** for a demonstration of the selected Screen saver.

Tip: Tap **Settings** next to a feature for additional options.

Reduce animations

Decrease certain motion effects, such as when opening apps.

- o From Settings, tap **Advanced features** > **Reduce animations** to enable the feature.

Lift to wake

Turn on the screen by lifting the device.

- From Settings, tap **Advanced features** > **Motions and gestures** > Lift to wake to enable this feature.

Double tap to wake

Turn on the screen by double-tapping instead of using the Side key.

- From Settings, tap **Advanced features** > **Motions and gestures** > **Double tap to wake** to enable this feature.

Smart stay

Smart stay uses the front camera to detect your face so that the screen stays on while you are looking at it.

- From Settings, tap **Advanced features** > **Motions and gestures** > **Smart stay**, and tap to enable the feature.

One-handed mode

You can change the screen layout to accommodate operating your device with one hand.

1. From Settings, tap **Advanced features** > **One-handed mode**.

2. Tap **Use One-handed mode** to enable the feature and select one of the following options:

- **Gesture**: Swipe down in the center of the bottom edge of the screen.

- **Button**: Tap ☐ **Home** two times in quick succession to reduce the display size.

Device maintenance

View the status of your device's battery, storage, and memory. You can also automatically optimize your device's system resources.

Quick optimization

- The quick optimization feature improves device performance through the following actions:

- Identifying apps that use excessive battery power and clearing unneeded items from memory.

- Deleting unnecessary files and closing apps running in the background.

- Scanning for malware.

To use the quick optimization feature:

o From Settings, tap **Device care** > **Optimize now.**

Battery

View how battery power is used for your various device activities.

o From Settings, tap **Device care** > Battery for options:

- **Battery usage**: View power usage by app and service.

- **Power mode**: Select a power mode to extend battery life.

- **App power management**: Configure battery usage for apps that are used infrequently.

- **Wireless PowerShare**: Enable wireless charging of supported devices with your device's battery.

- **Charging**: Enable the following options to support fast charging capabilities:

  – **Fast charging**

- **Fast wireless charging**

Storage

View the device storage and usage.

Device storage

Quickly optimize your device's storage, increasing available memory.

- From Settings, tap **Device care** > **Storage** > **Clean now**

Memory

Check the amount of available memory. You can close background apps and reduce the amount of memory you are using to speed up your device.

- From Settings, tap **Device care** > **Memory**. The used and available memory are shown.

    - Tap **Clean now** to free up as much memory as possible.

    - Tap **View more** to view the full list of apps and services using memory. Tap to include or exclude these apps and services.

- Tap Apps not used recently to view apps and services that are included in this group. Tap ☑ to include or exclude these apps and services.

- Tap **Select apps to exclude** to choose apps to exclude from memory usage checks.

Advanced options

Other Device care features are available in the advanced menu.

- From Settings, tap ⟳ **Device care** > **More options** > **Advanced**. The following options are available:

    - **Notifications**: Enable or disable notifications from Device care.

    - **Auto optimization**: Automatically optimize the device daily.

        – **Time**: Choose a time of day to optimize the device.

        – **Close apps to free up memory**: Enable to free up memory by closing apps that are running in the background.

- **Auto restart**: Automatically restart the device on a custom schedule.
  - **Days**: Choose one or more days to restart the device.
  - **Time**: Choose a time of day to restart the device.
- **Optimize settings**: Save battery power by optimizing settings when the device is not in use.
  - **Brightness**: Reduce brightness.
  - **Screen timeout**: Turn off the screen after 30 seconds of inactivity.
  - **Media volume**: Limit playback volume to 46%.

Language and input

Configure your device's language and input settings.

Change the device language

You can add languages to your list and organize them according to preference. If an app does not support your default language, then it will move to the next supported language in your list.

1. From Settings, tap **General management** > **Language and input** > **Language**.

2. Tap **Add language**, and select a language from the list.

3. Tap **Set as default** to change the device language.

   - To switch to another language on the list, tap the desired language, and then tap Apply.

Default keyboard

You can select a default keyboard for your device's menus and keyboards. Additional keyboards can be downloaded from the Google Play store.

1. From Settings, tap **General management** > **Language and input**.

2. Tap **On-screen keyboard** > **Default keyboard** and choose a keyboard.

Google Voice typing

Speak rather than type your text entries using Google Voice™ typing.

1. From Settings, tap **General management** > **Language and input**.

2. Tap **On-screen keyboard** > **Google Voice typing** to customize settings.

Manage on-screen keyboards

Enable or disable on-screen keyboards.

1. From Settings, tap **General management** > **Language and input**.

2. Tap **On-screen keyboard** > Manage keyboards.

3. Tap each keyboard to enable or disable.

Show keyboard button

Show a button on the Navigation bar to quickly switch between keyboards.

1. From Settings, tap **General management** > **Language and input** > **On-screen keyboard**.

2. Tap Show keyboard button to enable this feature.

Physical keyboards

Customize options when you have a physical keyboard connected to your device (sold separately).

1. From Settings, tap **General management** > **Language and input**.
2. Tap **Physical keyboard**, and then choose an option:
    - **Show on-screen keyboard**: Show the on-screen keyboard while a physical keyboard is also being used.
    - **Keyboard shortcuts**: Show explanations of the keyboard shortcuts on the screen.
    - **Change language shortcut**: Enable or disable language key shortcuts for your physical keyboard.

Autofill service

Save time entering information using autofill services.

1. From Settings, tap ≡ **General Management** > **Language and input**.

2. Tap **Autofill service** and select your preferred service.

Text-to-speech

Configure your Text-to-Speech (TTS) options. TTS is used for various accessibility features, such as Voice Assistant.

- From Settings, tap ≡ **General management** > **Language and input>Text-to-speech** for options:

    - **Preferred engine**: Choose either the Samsung or Google Text-to-speech engine. Tap Settings for options.

    - **Language**: Set the default speech language.

    - **Speech rate**: Set the speed at which the text is spoken.

    - **Pitch**: Set the pitch of the speech.

    - **Play**: Tap to play a short demonstration of speech synthesis.

- **Reset:** Reset the speech rate and pitch.

Pointer speed

Configure pointer speed for an optional mouse or trackpad (not included).

1. From Settings, tap **General management** > **Language and input**.
2. Under Pointer speed, drag the slider to the right to go faster or to the left to go slower.

Primary mouse button

You can define which mouse button that you favor as primary.

1. From Settings, tap **General management** > **Language and input**.
2. Tap **Primary mouse button**, and choose either **Left** or Right.

Date and time

By default, your device receives date and time information from the wireless network. Outside of network coverage, you can set the date and time manually.

- From Settings, tap **General management** > **Date and time**. The following options are available:

    - **Automatic date and time**: Receive date and time updates from your wireless network. When Automatic date and time is disabled, the following options are available:

        – **Select time zone**: Choose a new time zone.

        – **Set date**: Enter the current date. – Set time: Enter the current time.

    - **Use 24-hour format**: Set the format for displaying time.

Troubleshooting

You can check for software updates and, if necessary, reset services on your device.

Software update

Check for and install available software updates for your device.

- From Settings, tap **Software update** for the following options:

- **Download and install**: Check for software updates and install if any are available.

- **Auto download over Wi-Fi**: Automatically download software updates when the device is connected to a Wi-Fi network.

- **Last update**: View information about the installation of the current software.

Reset

Device and network settings. You can also reset your device to its factory defaults.

Reset settings

You can reset your device to its factory default settings, which resets everything except the security, language, and account settings. Personal data is not affected.

1. From Settings, tap **General management** > **Reset** > **Reset settings**.

2. Tap **Reset settings**, and confirm when prompted.

Reset network settings

You can reset Wi-Fi, mobile data, and Bluetooth settings with Reset network settings.

1. From Settings, tap **General management** > **Reset** > **Reset network settings**.

2. Tap **Reset settings**, and confirm when prompted.

Reset accessibility settings

You can reset device accessibility settings. Accessibility settings in downloaded apps and your personal data are not affected.

1. From Settings, tap **General management** > **Reset** > **Reset accessibility settings**.

2. Tap **Reset settings**, and confirm when prompted.

Auto restart

Optimize your device by restarting it automatically at set times. Any unsaved data will be lost when the device restarts.

1. From Settings, tap **General management** > **Reset** > **Auto restart**.

2. Tap to activate Auto restart, and then set the following parameters:

- **Days**: Select the day of the week to automatically restart your device.

- **Time:** Set the time of day to restart your device.

Factory Data Reset

You can reset your device to factory defaults, erasing all data from your device. This action permanently erases ALL data from the device, including Google or other account settings, system and application data and settings, downloaded applications, as well as your music, photos, videos, and other files.

When you sign in to a Google Account on your device, Factory Reset Protection (FRP) is activated. This protects your device in the event it is lost or stolen.

If you reset your device to factory default settings with the FRP feature activated, you must enter the user name and password for a registered Google Account to regain access to the device. You will not be able to access the device without the correct credentials.

Note: If you reset your Google Account password, it can take 24 hours for the password reset to sync with all devices registered to the account.

Before resetting your device:

1. Verify that the information you want to keep has transferred to your storage area.

2. Log in to your Google Account and confirm your user name and password.

To reset your device:

1. From Settings, tap General management > Reset > Factory data reset.

2. Tap Reset and follow the prompts to perform the reset.

3. When the device restarts, follow the prompts to set up your device.

Factory Reset Protection

When you sign in to a Google Account on your device, Factory Reset Protection (FRP) is activated. FRP prevents other people from using your device if it is reset to factory settings without your permission. For example, if your device is lost or stolen and a factory data reset is performed, only someone with your Google Account username and password can use the device.

You will not be able to access the device after a factory data reset if you do not have your Google Account username and password.

Caution: Before sending your device to Samsung or taking it to a Samsung authorized service center, remove your Google Account and then perform a factory data reset.

Enable Factory Reset Protection

Adding a Google Account to your device automatically activates the FRP security feature.

Disable Factory Reset Protection

To disable FRP, remove all Google Accounts from the device.

1. From Settings, tap 🔑 **Accounts and backup** > **Accounts** > [Google Account].
2. Tap Remove account.

Lock screen and security

You can secure your device and protect your data by setting a screen lock.

Screen lock types

You can choose from the following screen lock types that offer high, medium, or no security: Swipe, Pattern, PIN, Password, and None.

Note: Biometric locks are also available to protect access to your device and sensitive data on your device.

Set a secure screen lock

It is recommended that you secure your device using a secure screen lock (Pattern, PIN, or Password). This is necessary to set up and enable biometric locks.

1. From Settings, tap **Lock screen** > **Screen lock type** and tap a secure screen lock (**Pattern, PIN, or Password**).

2. Tap to enable showing notifications on the lock screen. The following options are available:

    - **View style**: Display notification details or hide them and show only an icon.

- **Hide content**: Do not show notifications in the Notification panel.

- **Notifications to show**: Choose which notifications to show on the Lock screen.

- **Show on Always On Display**: Display notifications on the Always on Display screen.

3. Tap **Done** when finished.

4. Configure the following screen lock options:

- **Smart Lock**: Unlock your device automatically when trusted locations or other devices have been detected. A secure screen lock is required for this feature.

- **Secure lock settings**: Customize your secure lock settings. A secure screen lock is required for this feature.

Clock and information

You can configure features that appear on the Lock screen, like the clock and other useful information.

- From Settings, tap 🔒 **Lock screen** for the following options:

  - **Wallpaper services**: Enable additional features such as guide page and Dynamic Lock Screen.

  - **Clock style**: Set the type and color of the clock on the Lock screen and Always On Display screen.

  - **Roaming clock**: Change to digital clocks showing both local and home time zones when roaming.

  - **FaceWidgets**: Enable widgets on the Lock screen and Always on Display screen to get quick access to useful information.

  - **Contact information**: Show your contact information, such as your phone number or email address.

  - **Notifications**: Select which notifications to display on the Lock screen and Always On Display screen.

- **Shortcuts**: Select which app shortcuts to add to the Lock screen.

- **About Lock screen**: Update the Lock screen's software.

Google Play Protect

You can configure Google Play to regularly check your apps and device for security risks and threats.

- From Settings, tap **Biometrics and security** > **Google Play Protect**.

- Updates are checked for automatically.

Find My Mobile

You can protect your device from loss or theft by allowing your device to be locked, tracked online, and for your data to be deleted remotely. A Samsung account is required, and Google location service must be turned on in order to use Find My Mobile.

Turn on Find My Mobile

Before you can use the Find My Mobile feature, you must turn it on and customize the options.

1. From Settings, tap **Biometrics and security** > **Find My Mobile**.

2. Tap to enable Find My Mobile and log in to your Samsung account. The following options are available:

    - **Remote unlock**: Allow Samsung to store your PIN, pattern, or password, allowing you to unlock and control your device remotely.

    - **Send last location**: Allow your device to send its last location to the Find My Mobile server when the remaining battery charge falls below a certain level.

Security update

You can easily check the date of the last installed security software update and find out if newer updates are available.

   - From Settings, tap **Biometrics and security** > **Security update** to see the latest security update installed and check if a newer update is available

Samsung Pass

Use Samsung Pass to access your favorite services with biometric data. You must sign in to your Samsung account to use Samsung Pass.

1. From Settings, tap **Biometrics and security** > **Samsung Pass**.

2. Sign in to your Samsung account and add your biometric data.

Samsung Blockchain Keystore

Manage your blockchain private key.

1. From Settings, tap **Biometrics and security** > **Samsung Blockchain Keystore**.

2. Follow the prompts to import or set up a new cryptocurrency wallet.

Install unknown apps

You can allow installation of unknown third-party apps from selected apps or sources.

1. From Settings, tap **Biometrics and security** > **Install unknown apps**.

2. Tap an app or source, and then tap Allow from this source.

Tip: Installing unknown third-party apps could make your device and personal data more vulnerable to security risks.

Secure Folder

You can create a secure folder on your device to protect private content and apps from anyone who may be using your device. You must sign in to your Samsung account to set up and use secure folder.

- o From Settings, tap **Biometrics and security** > **Secure Folder** and follow the prompts to secure content on your device.

Secure Wi-Fi

Get extra privacy protection while using unsecured Wi-Fi networks. You must sign in to your Samsung account to set up and use Secure Wi-Fi.

- o From Settings, tap **Biometrics and security** > **Secure Wi-Fi** and follow the prompts to configure privacy protection.

View passwords

You can have characters displayed briefly in password fields as you type them.

- From Settings, tap **Biometrics and security > Other security settings > Make passwords visible** to turn on the feature.

Device administration

You can authorize security features and apps (like Find My Mobile) to have administrative access to your device.

1. From Settings, tap **Biometrics and security > Other security settings > Device admin apps**.

2. Tap an option to turn it on as a device administrator.

Credential storage

You can manage the trusted security certificates installed on your device, which verify the identity of servers for secure connections.

- From Settings, tap **Biometrics and security > Other security settings** for the following options:
    - **Storage type**: Select a storage location for credential contents.

- **View security certificates**: Display certificates in your device's ROM and other certificates you have installed.

- **User certificates**: View user certificates that identify your device.

- **Install from device storage**: Install a new certificate from storage.

- **Clear credentials**: Erase credential contents from the device and reset the password.

Advanced security settings

You can use these options to configure advanced security settings to better protect your device.

- From Settings, tap **Biometrics and security** > **Other security** settings for the following options:

    - **Trust agents**: Allow trusted devices to perform selected actions when connected.

        – This option is only displayed when a lock screen is turned on.

- **Pin windows**: Pin an app on your device screen, which prevents access to other features of your device.

- **Security policy updates**: Keep your device secure by checking for security updates.

Location

Location services use a combination of GPS, mobile network and Wi-Fi to determine the location of your device.

1. From Settings, tap **Location**.

2. Tap to turn on Location services.

Tip: Some apps require location services be turned on for full functionality.

App permissions

Configure permissions for apps that want to access your location information.

1. From Settings, tap **Location** > **App permissions**.

2. Tap an app and select which of the following location permissions to grant it:

- Allow all the time
- Allow only while using the app
- Deny

Improve accuracy

Enable other location scanning tools.

1. From Settings, tap **Location** > **Improve accuracy**.

2. Tap connection method to add or remove from location services:

- **Wi-Fi scanning**: Allow apps and services to scan for Wi-Fi networks automatically, even when Wi-Fi is turned off.

- **Bluetooth scanning**: Allow apps to scan for and connect to nearby devices automatically through Bluetooth, even when Bluetooth is turned off.

Recent location requests

View a list of apps that have requested your location.

1. From Settings, tap **Location**.

2. Tap to turn on Location services.

3. Tap an entry under **Recent location requests** to view the app's settings.

Location services

Location services store and use your device's most recent location data. Certain apps can use this data to improve your search results based on places that you have visited.

1. From Settings, tap **Location**.

2. Tap an entry under **Location services** to see how your location information is used.

Permission manager

Apps might access features of your device that you permit them to (like the camera, microphone, or location) when they are running in the background, not just when you are using the app. You can set your device to notify you when this happens.

1. From Settings, tap **Privacy** > **Permission manager.**

2. Tap a category, and then tap an app to select which permissions you want to be notified about by tapping Allow or Deny.

Note: When using an app or service for the first time that wants to access certain features of your device, a dialog box asks if you want to permit such access. You can choose from Allow all the time, Allow only while using the app, or Deny for each type of access requested.

Send diagnostic data

Send diagnostic information about your device to Samsung when you are having technical problems.

1. From Settings, tap **Privacy** > **Send diagnostic data**.

2. Read and accepts the consent information to enable this feature.

Accounts

You can connect to and manage your accounts, including your Google Account, Samsung account, email, and social networking accounts.

Samsung Cloud

You can keep your data safe by backing up and restoring your device. You can also sync your data from multiple devices.

1. From Settings, tap 🔑 **Accounts and backup** > **Samsung Cloud**.

- If a Samsung account has not been added, the screens explain how to create or sign in to your account.

2. Once a Samsung account is configured, you can view and manage items stored in the Samsung Cloud.

Add an account

You can add and sync all your email, social networking, and picture and video sharing accounts.

1. From Settings, tap 🔑 **Accounts and backup** > **Accounts** > ➕ **Add account**.

2. Tap one of the account types.

3. Follow the prompts to enter your credentials and set up the account.

- Tap **Auto sync data** to enable automatic updates to your accounts.

Account settings

Each account has its own custom settings. You can configure common settings for all accounts of the same type. Account settings and available features vary between account types.

1. From Settings, tap 🔑 **Accounts and backup** > **Accounts**.

2. Tap an account to configure that account's sync settings.

3. Tap other available options for the account type.

Remove an account

You can remove accounts from your device.

1. From Settings, tap 🔑 **Accounts and backup** > **Accounts**.

2. Tap the account and then tap Remove account.

Backup and restore

You can configure your device to back up data to your personal accounts.

Samsung account

You can enable backup of your information to your Samsung account.

- From Settings, tap 🔑 **Accounts and backup** > Backup and restore for options:

• **Back up data**: Configure your Samsung account to back up your data.

• **Restore data**: Use your Samsung account to restore your backup data.

Google Account

You can enable backup of your information to your Google Account.

- From Settings, tap 🔑 **Accounts and backup** > **Backup and restore** for options:

• **Back up my data**: Enable back up of application data, Wi-Fi passwords, and other settings to Google servers.

- **Backup account**: Select a Google Account to be used as your backup account.

- **Automatic restore**: Enable automatic restoration of settings from Google servers.

External storage transfer

You can back up your data to a USB storage device, or restore backup data using Smart Switch.

- From Settings, tap **Accounts and backup** > **Backup and restore** > **External storage transfer**.

Google settings

You can configure your device's Google settings. Available options depend on your Google Account.

- From Settings, tap **Google**, and select an option to customize.

Chapter 7

Accessibility

There are accessibility settings for people who need help seeing, hearing, or otherwise operating their device. Accessibility services are special features that make using the device easier for everyone

Screen Reader

Use special controls and settings that let you navigate without needing to see the screen.

- From Settings, tap 🯅 **Accessibility** > **Screen reader** and tap an option:

  • **Voice assistant**: Receive spoken feedback when using your device, such as what you touch, select, or activate.

  • **Tutorial**: Lean how to use Voice assistant.

  • **Settings**: Configure Voice assistant to better assist you.

Visibility enhancements

You can configure Accessibility features to assist with visual aspects of your device.

Colors and clarity

You can adjust the colors and contrast of text and other screen elements for easier viewing.

- From Settings, tap 🯄 **Accessibility** > **Visibility enhancements** and tap an option:
  - **High contrast theme**: Adjust colors and screen fonts to increase the contrast for easier viewing.
  - **High contrast fonts**: Adjust the color and outline of fonts to increase the contrast with the background.
  - **High contrast keyboard**: Adjust the size of the Samsung keyboard and change its colors to increase the contrast between the keys and the background.
  - **Show button shapes**: Show buttons with shaded backgrounds to make them stand out better against the wallpaper.
  - **Color inversion**: Reverse the display of colors from white text on a black background to black text on a white background.

- **Color adjustment**: Adjust the color of the screen if you find it difficult to see some colors.

- **Color lens**: Adjust the screen colors if you have difficulty reading the text.

- **Remove animations**: Remove certain screen effects if you are sensitive to motion.

Size and zoom

You can increase the size of supported screen elements and create shortcuts for accessibility features on your device.

- o From Settings, tap 🯂 **Accessibility** > **Visibility enhancements** and tap an option:

- **Magnifier window**: Magnify content shown on the screen.

- **Magnification**: Use exaggerated gestures such as triple-tapping, double pinching, and dragging two fingers across the screen.

- **Large mouse/touchpad pointer**: Use a large pointer for a connected mouse or touchpad (accessories not included).

- **Font size and style**: Configure screen fonts.

- **Screen zoom**: Configure the screen zoom level.

Hearing enhancements

You can configure Accessibility features to assist with audial aspects of the device.

Sounds

You can adjust audio quality when using hearing aids or earphones.

- From Settings, tap 🯄 **Accessibility** > **Hearing enhancements** and tap an option:

- **Hearing aid support**: Improve the sound quality to work better with hearing aids.

- **Amplify ambient sound**: Enable this feature and connect headphones to your device to amplify the sounds of conversations.

- **Adapt sound**: Customize the sound for each ear and enhance your listening experience.

- **Left/right sound balance**: Use the slider to adjust the left and right balance when listening to audio in stereo.

- **Mono audio**: Switch audio from stereo to mono when using one earphone.

- **Mute all sounds**: Turn off all notifications and audio for privacy.

Text display

You can watch closed captions when viewing multimedia.

- From Settings, tap **Accessibility** > **Hearing enhancements** and tap an option:
- **Live transcribe**: Use the microphone to record speech and convert it to text.
- **Live caption**: Automatically caption speech in media played on your device.
- **Subtitle settings**: Configure closed caption and subtitle services.
- **Sound detectors**: Receive alerts when the device detects a baby crying or a doorbell.

Interaction and dexterity

You can configure Accessibility features to assist with limited dexterity when interacting with your device.

Alternate input

You can control your device using different kinds of inputs and controls.

- ○ From Settings, tap **⚹Accessibility** > **Interaction and dexterity** and tap an option:

  - **Universal switch**: Control your device with your customized switches.

  - **Assistant menu**: Improve device accessibility for users with reduced dexterity.

Interactions

You can simplify the motions needed to answer phone calls or respond to notifications and alarms.

- ○ From Settings, tap **⚹Accessibility** > **Interaction and dexterity** and tap an option:

- **Answering and ending calls**: – Read caller names aloud: Hear callers' names read aloud when using Bluetooth or headsets (not included).

  – **Answer automatically**: Answer calls after a set duration when using Bluetooth or headsets (not included).

  – **Press Volume up to answer**: Use the Volume keys to answer calls.

  – **Press Side key to end calls**: End calls by pressing the Side key.

  – **Open phone to answer**: Open the device to answer an incoming call.

  – **Close phone to end**: Close the device to end a call.

- **Interaction control**: Customize areas of screen interactions, hardkeys, and the keyboard.

Touch settings

You can adjust your screen to be less sensitive to taps and touches.

- From Settings, tap 👤 **Accessibility** > **Interaction and dexterity** and tap an option:

- **Touch and hold delay**: Select a time interval for this action.

- **Tap duration**: Set how long an interaction must be held to be recognized as a tap.

- **Ignore repeated touches**: Set time duration in which to ignore repeated touches.

Mouse and physical keyboard

Configure settings for a connected mouse and physical keyboard.

- From Settings, tap 👤 **Accessibility** > **Interaction and dexterity** and tap an option:

- **Click after pointer stops**: Automatically click on an item after the pointer stops over it.

- **Sticky keys**: When you press a modifier key like Shift, Ctrl, or Alt, the key stays pressed down, which allows you to enter keyboard shortcuts by pressing one key at a time.

- **Slow keys**: Set how long a key must be held before it is recognized as a press, which helps avoid accidental key presses.

- **Bounce keys**: Set how long to wait before accepting a second press from the same key, which helps avoid accidentally, pressing the same key multiple times.

Advanced settings

You can customize additional accessibility features and services for your device.

Tip: Additional accessibility apps may be downloaded from the Google Play store.

Direct access

- From Settings, tap 👤 **Accessibility** > **Advanced settings** and tap an option:
- **Side and Volume up keys**: Configure selected Accessibility features to open by quickly pressing the Side and Volume up keys at the same time. Tap to enable the feature, and then tap any of the listed

Accessibility features to either enable or open the feature's menu.

- **Volume up and down keys**: Configure selected services to turn on when you press and hold the Volume up and Volume down keys for three seconds.

   - **Selected service**: Choose a service to launch with this key combination.

   - **Allow on Lock screen**: Allow this key combination to activate even when the screen is locked.

Notifications

- o From Settings, tap 🧍 **Accessibility** > **Advanced settings** and tap an option:

- **Flash notification**: Flash either the camera light or the screen when you receive notifications or when alarms sound.

- **Notification reminders**: Set periodic reminders for any unread notifications.

- **Time to take action**: Choose how long to show messages that ask you to take action, but are visible only temporarily (like notifications).

- **Voice Label**: Write voice recordings to NFC tags (not included) to provide you with information about objects or locations as you near them.

- **Bixby Vision for accessibility**: Add modes to read text aloud describe scenes, detect colors, and more.

Installed services

You can install additional assistance services for your device.

- From Settings, tap 🧍 **Accessibility** > **Installed services**.

Note: Additional accessibility services are listed and configured here after they are installed.

About Accessibility

Legal and license information about the current Accessibility software is available in Settings.

- From Settings, tap **Accessibility** > **About Accessibility**. The following information is available:

- **Version**: View the current Accessibility software version.

- **Legal information**: View Legal information for select Accessibility features.

- **Open source licenses**: View information for the open source licenses used for Accessibility.

Other settings

Configure features on your device that make it easier to use.

Tips and help

View tips and techniques as well as the user manual for your device.

- From Settings, tap **Tips and help**.

  - **What's new**: Explore the new features of your Galaxy device.

- **Smart ideas**: View tips for getting the most from your device.

- **Help**: View your device's user manual.

Dual Messenger

Use two separate accounts for the same app.

1. From Settings, tap **Advanced features** > **Dual Messenger**.

2. Tap next to supported apps to enable the feature for each app.

    - To select which contacts have access to the secondary messenger app, tap **Use separate contacts list.**

About phone

View information about your device, including current status, legal information, hardware and software versions, and more.

1. From Settings, tap **About phone**, and then view your phone number, model number, serial number, and IMEI information.

2. Tap additional items to view more information about your device.

Tip: You can view your device's FCC ID from **About phone** > **Status**.

Chapter 8

Tips & Tricks

Hide Apps

The Samsung Galaxy S20 Ultra has a hidden space available to hide apps. You can hide certain apps that you want to keep private from snoopy eyes. You can also unhide apps whenever you feel it's not necessary anymore.

To access hidden space feature on Samsung devices, Tap and hold on Home Screen >> Settings >> Hide Apps. Now, you can select any app that you would like to hide. If you want to unhide any app just unselect it in the Hide Apps option.

Hide Front Cameras

The Samsung Galaxy S20 Ultra has a punch-hole camera in the top middle and it might bother you while watching YouTube videos or movies on the device. Thankfully, there is an option available to hide it.

If you want to hide the front camera, Go to Settings >> Display >> Full-screen apps >> Hide front camera and turn on the option. If you turn this option on it will insert a little black bar to the top of the screen so the front camera won't be visible.

In-Display Ultrasonic Fingerprint Scanner

Samsung Galaxy S20 Ultra comes with an in-display ultrasonic fingerprint scanner. The fingerprint reader is fast and accurate, it unlocks your smartphone by putting the thumb on the lock screen.

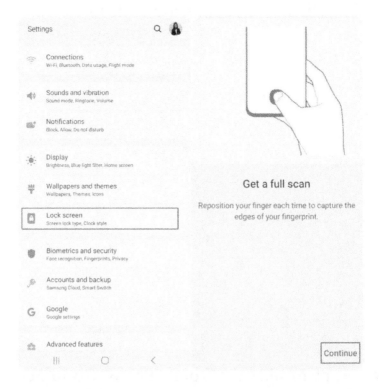

The ultrasonic fingerprint scanner is a must-use feature of this phone. To set a fingerprint lock on S20 Ultra, Go to

Settings >> Biometrics and Security >> Fingerprints >> Add fingerprint and register your fingerprint.

Assistant Menu

This feature is made for individuals with physical impairments or motor control. By enabling the Assistant menu option, you can access all the physical buttons and every part of the screen by just swiping or tapping.

If you want to enable the Assistant Menu, Go to Home screen >> Settings >> Accessibility >> Tap on Interaction and Dexterity option. Now, just turn on the Assistant Menu option.

Reverse Wireless Charging

Samsung Galaxy S20 Ultra can wirelessly charge devices that support wireless charging. For example, charging Galaxy Buds or Galaxy Smartwatch using the Galaxy S20 Ultra. The Wireless PowerShare feature will be helpful for those who want to keep their devices charged on the go without a wireless charger.

If you want to charge devices using the Galaxy S20 Ultra, open the notification panel and tap on Wireless PowerShare button. Now, flip the phone and put the devices on the back of the phone that you want to charge.

Battery Percentage In Status Bar

By default, the battery percentage does not show in the status bar. You have to turn on this option from the settings to make the percentage appear in the status bar.

To enable this on your Samsung Galaxy S20 Ultra, Go to Settings >> Notifications >> Status Bar, and toggle on the "Show Battery Percentage" option. By enabling this option the remaining battery percentage of the device will be shown on the left side of the battery icon.

One-Handed Mode

The S20 Ultra has a huge 6.9-inch display, and it is hard for many users to navigate the phone using one hand. But, there a solution available for it provided in OneUI, you can use the Samsung Galaxy S20 Ultra in one-handed mode. This feature will shrink the screen size as per your requirement.

To enable the one-hand mode, Head to Settings >> Advanced Features >> Motion and Gestures >> One-handed mode, and turn on the option.

Hide Albums In Gallery

There is another cool feature in S20 Ultra, you can hide photos and albums in the Gallery. This feature comes in handy to keep people away from checking out your private photos and videos.

If you want to use this feature then, Open the Gallery app >> Tap on the three dots in the top right corner >> Tap 'Hide or Unhide albums' option. Now, select the albums you want to hide, the selected albums won't be visible in the gallery until you unhide them.

Dual Messenger

Dual Messenger feature can be found in most of the smartphones nowadays including Xiaomi, Realme, Vivo, and Oppo. The Dual Messenger feature to let you use more than one account for a similar app like WhatsApp or Snapchat. This feature is available on Galaxy S20 Ultra too.

To enable this feature, Go to Settings >> Advanced features >> Dual Messenger, and select the apps you want to clone.

Use Edge Screen

The Samsung Galaxy S20 Ultra comes with an edge display. Using the edge display you can access the edge shortcuts by simply swiping the Edge panel. To view, the edge shortcuts drag the edge panel handle. There is one another amazing feature available called Edge lighting whenever you receive a notification the edges of the phone glows.

To enable this feature, Go to Settings >> Display >> Edge screen, and customize the panels as per your requirement.

Swipe Palm To Take Screenshot

OneUI gives you a set of useful gestures so that you can easily perform actions. You can take a screenshot on S20 Ultra by swiping your Palm on the edge across the screen, It is a great alternative to the default way of taking a screenshot.

To activate this feature, Head to Settings >> Advanced Features >> Motion and Gestures >> Palm Swipe to Capture, and turn on the option.

Take Photos With Palm

You can take photos on S20 Ultra without tapping the shutter button, It automatically takes photos when you show your Palm to the camera. This feature comes in handy whenever you are not able to reach the shutter button, you just have to show your palm to the camera and it will take the photo.

To activate this feature, Go to Camera >> Camera Settings >> Shooting methods >> Show Palm, and enable the option.

Navigation Gestures

The navigation gestures on S20 Ultra will help you to get rid of the navigation bar, and free up small space on your screen. These gestures offer you to navigate the interface more intuitively.

To enable the Navigation Gestures, Go to Settings >> Display >> Navigation Bar, and select the Full-screen gestures option.

Double Tap To Wake Up

The Ambient Display feature in S20 Ultra shows you a preview of your notifications, battery percentage and date and time. Also, you can wake the phone using the ultrasonic fingerprint scanner or face unlock. However, the double-tap to wake feature comes in handy when you want to wake the screen using the power key.

To activate Double Tap to Wake Up, Go to Settings >> Advanced Features >> Motion and Gestures >> Double tap to wake up, and enable the option.

Enable Flashlight Notifications

The Flashlight notifications feature is really helpful when your phone is on silent mode and you are in a movie theatre or a dark environment. This feature notifies by flashing the LED whenever you receive calls and messages.

To enable this feature, Head to Settings >> Accessibility >> Advanced settings >> Flashlight notification, and enable the Camera flash and Screen flash option.

Power & Volume Keys Shortcut

In Galaxy S20 Ultra using the Power and Volume Keys, you can quickly access to the accessibility settings. These keys can be used to access multiple accessibility features like magnification, voice assistant, and more available on the device.

To enable this feature, Go to Settings >> Accessibility >> Advanced settings >> Power and Volume Up keys, and toggle on the option.

Enable Dark Mode(Night Mode)

Samsung Galaxy S20 Ultra comes with a built-in dark mode feature which enables dark theme all around the UI.

Apps like Contacts and Dialer are also forced to appear in dark mode.

To enable the dark mode, Go to Settings >> Display >> Night Mode. This option will help you by providing a little comfort to eyes at night.

Send Schedule Message

It's funny how a single missed message can wreak havoc in one's life. You need to send an important message to someone sometime later in the day, and you are so sure you will send it at the right time. Only, when the right time comes, you forget to send it. Depending upon the importance of the message you forgot to send, you may suffer anywhere from nothing to a concussion

- Open your Messaging app
- Then select your desired contact
- Then type a message as you like
- Then tap on "+" plus sign
- You will see the option Schedule Message tap on it
- Now set your time and date and press Done option and send.

Now you will little clock beside your message which means your message is scheduled.

Lockdown Mode

New in Samsung's One UI/Android Pie is an option to Lockdown your device. It's in the lock screen preferences option and can be toggled on with a quick tap. If you're ever in a situation where you don't want people to access your phone – possibly being faced with law enforcement wanting to access your phone – the button will disable facial recognition/Iris Scanner and your phones fingerprint sensor.

- In your mobile go to Settings
- Go to Lock Screen option
- Then go to the Secure Lock Settings
- Put your Pin/Pattern/Password
- Now you will see in last Show Lockdown Option
- Then activate the Lockdown mode.
- Now you press & hold the power button and choose the Lockdown Option to activate.

Keep in mind, if you activate Lockdown mode that turns off Smart Lock, biometrics unlock, and notification on the Lock Screen. #4. Assistant Menu The assistant menu is designed for individuals with motor control or other physical impairments. By using Assistant menu, you can access hardware buttons and all parts of the screen by simply tapping or swiping. If you want to Activate Assistant Menu, Follow these steps below-

- Go to your Home screen
- Tap on the Settings
- Scroll to Accessibility and tap on it
- Then tap on Interaction and dexterity

- And, then simply enable the Assistant Menu option.

Now as you know Assistant Menu is a contextual menu that appears on the screen. you can put it anywhere on the screen. You can tap on the Assistant Menu button it gives you some options like the Recents button, Home button, back button, Screen off, Volume, Screenshots and many more.

Pin Windows Feature

The Pin Windows feature is spinning an app it means opening an app and pinning it to the screen. This way it will not be accidentally closed because no button on the phone we close it, this will prevent others from using other features outside the app and also messages and calls are blocked when an app is pinned. In order to close the app you need to press and hold simmers down you see the back and recent apps soft buttons. To activate this Feature

- Go to the Settings
- Then Biometrics and security
- Tap on Other Security settings
- There will you find Pin windows

After that, if you want any app to be pinned just open it for normal use then press the recent app button press the app icon at the top and choose pin this app.

The Auto Restart Feature

Samsung's new UI brings so many unique features and the auto-restart feature move to the other setting.

- Go to your Home screen
- Tap on the Settings
- Scroll to Device Care
- Tap on three dots to the right top screen corner
- Tap on Auto Restart
- Choose your scheduled date and time. The defaults are Monday at 3 AM
- Turn on this feature and exit the menu

This allows to restart your phone once a week on a given day and a given time, which make sure that your phone runs are smoother fluid than normal so this option used to be in another part of the phone but now it's been moved under device care which more sense because you are caring for your device.

Lock Home Screen Layout

If you are using the One UI, you can avoid your home screen icons from being misplaced changing your settings. In a recent update in One UI, Samsung added few additional settings to lock your home screen layout. This will prevent your icons from misplacing on your home screen. On phones running the Android Pie-based Samsung One UI, users can now enable the "Lock Home screen layout" setting to prevent such accidents from happening.

- To activate this go to Settings
- Then Display
- Click the Home Screen menu
- You will found Lock Home Screen Layout
- Touch to enable it.

Now, if you try to move to drag anything from home screen it will stay as-is. By doing this you can make sure your icon setup is not disturbed by keeping your phone in your pocket or by accidentally pressing icons.

Lift to wake feature

With Lift to wake enabled, one can just bring the phone up to their face and have it automatically scan the eyes and unlock the phone, without requiring any button presses. Of course, it works just as well with Intelligent Scan, which scans both the eyes and the face for authentication. The Lift to wake feature is especially useful if you unlock your device via biometric options like Intelligent Scan or the iris sensor.

- Go to Settings menu on your device
- Click on Advanced features
- Then go to Motions and gestures
- You will find Lift to wake option

When you activate it you will be able to turn on the display by lifting the phone from the table or getting an out from your pocket without pressing any buttons.

Navigation Gestures

Samsung provided the on-screen navigation on the One UI with a new dimension. Not only can you hide the navigation bar – like on all recent Samsung phones – but you can keep navigating without removing the bar. Go to Display in the Settings, scroll down a bit and choose Navigation bar> Full-screen gestures option. To switch to gesture navigation, make sure the Show and Hide button is on, and choose the Actions for Start, Back and Recent option. Then, at the bottom left, tap the 'dot' that hides the navigation bar. Full-screen gestures, which requires you to swipe up from the bottom of the screen to go back, go to the home screen, or access the recent apps screen. Basically, you swipe up where these buttons would be placed in the navigation bar and weren't hidden.

Samsung Galaxy S20, S20+, and S20 Ultra: Camera features and Tips

Samsung Galaxy S20 introduces an entirely new camera system—powered by AI and with Samsung's biggest image sensor yet—to bring out the best in every image and every moment.

With a next-level smartphone like the Galaxy S20 Ultra, you have everything you need to shoot, edit and share incredible social content quickly and affordably.

The most dramatic change in the Galaxy S20 series is its innovative camera. The new and improved camera will make all of your photos stand out, whether you're aiming for a professional look or just want to take pictures for fun.

HERE IS WHAT COMES ON THE DIFFERENT MODELS:

All 3 versions: One front camera, and Wide and Ultra-Wide capabilities in the rear camera.

Galaxy S20 5G: A 10M selfie camera and 3 cameras on its back. The main lens is 12M, the telephoto lens is 64M (with 3x optical zoom), and the Ultra-Wide lens is 12M.

Galaxy S20+ 5G: A 10M selfie camera and 4 cameras on its back. The main lens is 12M, the telephoto lens is 64M (with 3x optical zoom), and the Ultra-Wide lens is 12M. It also has a Time of Flight sensor.

Galaxy S20 Ultra 5G: A 40MP selfie camera and 4 cameras on its back. The main lens is 108M, the telephoto lens is 48M (with 10x optical zoom), and the Ultra-Wide lens is 12M. It also has a Time of Flight sensor.

The S20 series' cameras are packed with new features that are simple to use and will take your video and selfie skills further. It's easier than ever to post exciting and personalized content to your favorite social media app with

Single take photos. Enable Night mode when shooting outside in the evening, and use advanced zoom from hundreds of feet away without sacrificing quality.

COMPARE CAMERA FEATURES

All Galaxy S20 series' front and rear cameras include Single Take for quick, 15-second clips and Space Zoom for magnifying objects near or far. Although you can capture incredible shots with each model, there are a few differences.

SINGLE TAKE: TAKE ONE SHOT, GET MULTIPLE FORMATS

You've heard of burst mode? Meet beast mode. With revolutionary AI, Single Take lets you shoot for up to 10 seconds and get back a variety of formats—meaning you can choose the best style for the moment without having to reshoot.

You can use Single Take to create photo clips of scenes, objects, and people. The camera's AI will decide which images to capture to make a video.

HOW TO USE GALAXY S20 SINGLE TAKE FEATURE:

To start the camera, navigate to and open the Camera app, and then tap SINGLE TAKE. Tap Capture. When Single Take is activated, the camera will utilize multiple functions at once, including Best Shot, Ultra-wide Shots, Live Focus, Filter, and Smart Crop. The videos will use motion photo, bounce and reverse, and Hyperlapse.

After you've taken your shots you can select a thumbnail, and then tap Favorite (the heart icon) to set it as your favorite of the bunch.

To access additional editing options with Single Take, touch and hold the thumbnail you'd like to edit. Tap Best shot (the crown icon) to set a clip as the best-looking photo. Tap Save to add the thumbnail to your Gallery and delete the rest. Tap Share to send your video or clips to friends or a social media app.

You can also create a movie by tapping Story Video Editor, and then choose from Highlight reel to show off the best moments from your clips, or Self-edited if you'd like to trim the video yourself. In Story Video Editor, you can customize your video by adding text or music.

When using Single Take, the camera will capture up to five photos and four videos, depending on how long you choose to record.

NIGHT MODE – BRIGHT NIGHT

The new Galaxy S20 phones also offer improved lowlight photography, stability, and zooming functions. If you need to take a selfie or video while out with your friends after dark, use Night mode for a vivid shot without any distortion.

In low light, the pro-grade camera system captures multiple photos at once, merging them into one stunning shot with minimal blur and noise. With larger image sensors and AI, switching to Night Mode means you can shoot luminous nighttime scenes without flash, even in low light.

Pull off those large group selfies with steady capture that offers smooth images every time. When filming a video, you can turn on the improved Super Steady feature to help keep images as clear as possible. The frame will remain steady no matter how you're holding your phone.

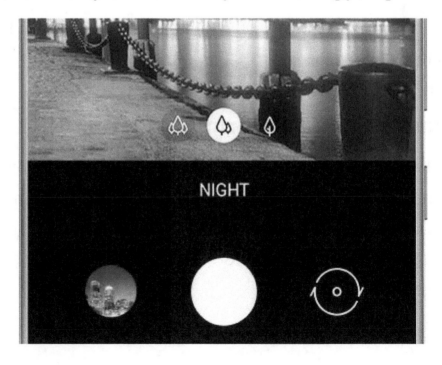

ZOOM:

With the Galaxy S20's Space Zoom technology, even when you are far away, you can zoom in close. Use up to 30x zoom on the Galaxy S20 and S20+ with Space Zoom, our AI-based Super-Resolution Zoom, or step- up to 100x Space Zoom, with the revolutionary folded lens on the S20 Ultra with 10x Hybrid Optic Zoom.

You can zoom in from at least 100 feet away using the Galaxy S20 5G and Galaxy S20+ 5G models and still capture the details on your subject. Use the Galaxy S20 Ultra 5G's advanced zoom while standing 300 feet away and still get that perfect, clear shot.

Once you've taken your photo, tap the Edit icon to crop it. Touch and drag the corners of the photo until you are finished cropping, and then tap Save.

8K VIDEO

Get the highest-resolution video on a smartphone. Samsung has revolutionized the resolution for mobile video, taking it from 4K all the way to 8K. That's 4 times bigger than UHD and 16 times bigger than HD. That's right, moving images that keep their super-sharp resolution even on your Samsung TV screen.

The Galaxy S20 offers stunning 8K video shooting, so users can capture their world in true-to-life color and quality. When you are done shooting, stream your video to a Samsung QLED 8K TV and enjoy a best-in-class viewing experience or grab a still from an 8K video and turn it into a high-res photo. And even the bumpiest videos look like they were shot using an action cam, thanks to Super Steady and its anti-rolling stabilization and AI motion analysis.

PRO MODE

Craft your content with a pro-grade tool set made for masters. Control the way you capture with the options at your fingertips in Pro Mode. Just like on a DSLR, you can manually adjust settings like ISO, shutter speed and exposure level to your heart's content.

MY FILTERS

Use the My Filters feature to create your own filters for your photos or videos. Take an existing photo that you like, and apply the colors and styles to another photo as you capture it.

If you've seen another photo with an effect that you admire, just add it to your Gallery and use it to make your own filter. Up to 99 custom filters can be created and saved to your phone.

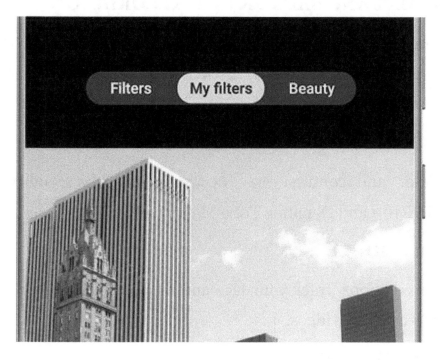

And all the favorites that set new standards

HDR

Shoot photos and videos with brilliant, true-to-life hues.

PHOTO AND VIDEO BOKEH

Blur out backgrounds and add bokeh effects for artistic photos and videos.

SUPER SLOW-MO

The super-speed camera shoots up to 960 frames per second.10

FRONT AND BACK 4K UHD RECORDING

Both front and rear cameras shoot in stunning 4K UHD, and you can seamlessly switch between the two while recording.

HDR10+ RECORDING

Color and contrast stay accurate in each scene with HDR10+ and Dynamic Tone Mapping.

AR DOODLE

3D creations track your face and the space around you for eye-catching videos.

3D SCANNER

Turn real-life objects into 3D animations.

QUICK MEASURE

It's a measuring device on your camera.

Every zoom option and features available on the Galaxy S20, S20+, and S20 Ultra

SAMSUNG GALAXY S20 5G AND S20+ 5G: TRUE ZOOM FEATURE

Samsung Galaxy S20 5G and Galaxy S20+ 5G cameras include a True Zoom function that will take clear, crisp photos from 100 feet away. It will feel like you're only 3 feet away with the 30x zoom, it will allow advanced zooming.

HOW TO USE GALAXY S20 TRUE ZOOM FEATURE:

You can start the True Zoom feature by opening the Camera app and tapping Photo. Pinch your fingers on the screen to zoom in. You can also slide your finger along the bottom to increase and decrease the zoom. You may need to steady the phone for a few seconds to allow the frame to come into focus. Once you've zoomed in, tap Capture.

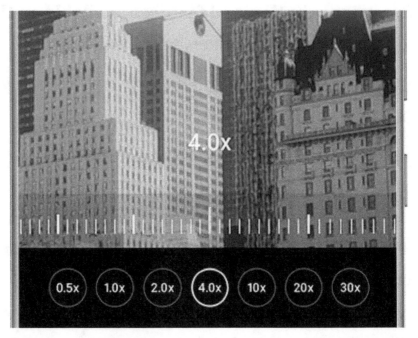

SAMSUNG GALAXY S20 ULTRA SUPER OPTIC ZOOM:

Samsung Galaxy S20 Ultra 5G camera features a Super Optic Zoom, which is capable of capturing images from an incredible 330 feet away. You can magnify the details of an object up close as well.

HOW TO USE GALAXY S20 ULTRA SUPER OPTIC ZOOM FEATURE:

To use the Super Optic Zoom on your Galaxy S20 Ultra 5G, open the Camera app, and then tap Photo. You can tap the three zoom icons at the bottom of the screen, or pinch your fingers to zoom in. Tap the additional options to test out the different zoom capacities. The strongest zoom available is 100x, which will take detailed photos from far away.

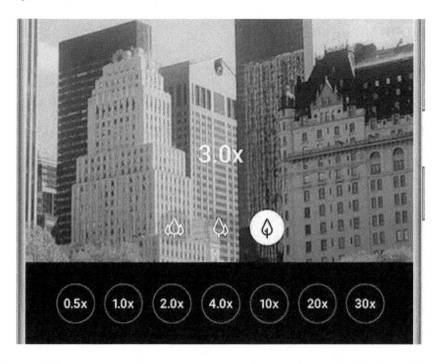

Note: When zooming in past 10x, a picture of the object will appear in the corner of the screen. You can use this as a guide when zooming in on the person or object you wish to capture. This is especially helpful when zooming in from an extreme distance to help you get that flawless shot.

HOW TO CROP YOUR PHOTOS:

After taking a super zoomed-in photo, you can crop it however you like and still retain the photo's quality. This is due to the camera's high resolution, which will preserve your original photo.

Just navigate to and open the Gallery app, and then select the photo you want to crop. Then tap the Edit icon, and touch and drag the corners of the photo to resize it to your liking. Once you've found the correct size, tap Save. You can also tap Reset if you need to start over. Your newly cropped photo will be added to your Gallery next to the original photo.

You can also switch between the photos to see the cropped and uncropped versions. You can continue cropping by selecting the photo, and then tapping Edit again.

Check out the 100x Space Zoom of Samsung Galaxy S20 Ultra

The Galaxy S20 and S20+ have a 64MP camera, while the Galaxy S20 Ultra has a 108MP camera. The benefit is that the larger sensors take in more light, so you get rich image quality even in low light situations.

The Galaxy S20 Ultra takes things a step further with the option to shift dynamically between a high-resolution

108MP mode and a 12MP mode, thanks to nona-binning technology which combines nine pixels into one at the sensor level.

There is a groundbreaking zoom capability. With the Galaxy S20's Space Zoom technology, even when you are far away, you can zoom in close.

Use up to 30x zoom on the Galaxy S20 and S20+ with Space Zoom, our AI-based Super-Resolution Zoom, or step- up to 100x Space Zoom, with the revolutionary folded lens on the S20 Ultra with 10x Hybrid Optic Zoom.

Thanks for purchasing our guide

Index

8

8K VIDEO 269

A

Access Settings 153
Accessibility 226
Accounts 221
Alarm 107
Always On Display. 44, 45, 86, 146, 189, 211
App settings 97, 98, 179
Apps panel 56
AR Zone 100
Assistant Menu 243
Auto restart 205
Auto Restart 260
Autofill service 200

B

Battery 194
Bixby 18, 41, 42, 43, 85, 97, 100, 236
Blue light filter 187
Bluetooth 158
Browser tabs 121

C

Calculator 103
Calendar 103
Call & text 52
Calls 129
Camera and Gallery 73
camera screen 74
Camera settings 80
charger 12, 180, 244
Contacts 113
Create movie 90

D

Dark mode 185
Dark Mode 255
Data usage 164
Date and time 202
Device storage 195
Digital wellbeing 43
Dolby Atmos 180
Download apps 94
Dual audio 160
Dual Messenger 238, 247

E

Easy mode 35, 36
Easy mute 176
Edge Screen 248
Edit pictures 86
Emergency alerts 125
Emergency mode 69, 70, 71, 72
Ethernet 173

F

Face recognition 46, 47
Factory Data Reset 206
File groups 127
Find My Mobile 212
Fingerprint scanner............................. 48
Fingerprint Scanner 242
Flashlight Notifications.................... 253
folders 95
Font size and style 188
Full screen apps 189

G

Gallery 84
Google Play Protect 212
Google Voice typing 199

H

Hearing enhancements 229
Hide Albums In Gallery 246
Hide Apps 240
Hide Front Cameras 241
Home screen 23, 25, 41, 46, 94, 96, 129, 130, 146, 243, 258, 260, 261

I

Installed services 236
Interaction and dexterity 231
Internet 120

L

Language and input 197
Link to Windows 51, 52
Live focus 75, 78, 79, 80
Location 218
Lockdown Mode 257

M

Manage calls 134
Memory 195
Messages 51, 124, 125, 126
MirrorLink 171
Mobile hotspot **166**
Multi window 53, 54, 55, 56
Multitask 133
MY FILTERS 270

N

Navigation ... 20, 25, 104, 105, 144, 252, 262, 263
NIGHT MODE 267
Notification panel 15, 37, 38, 39, 70, 133, 210
Notifications 183

O

One-handed mode 192
One-Handed Mode 246

P

parental controls 43
Phone 129
Pin Windows..................................... 259
Places 134
Play video... 87
Pointer speed...................................202
pop-up....25, 43, 52, 131, 132, 133, 134, 185
Power & Volume Keys...................... 254
Power off...............................15, 18, 40
PowerShare.......................12, 13, 244
PRO MODE 270

Q

Quick optimization............................193

R

Record videos 78, 80
Reduce animations........................... 191
Reset 204
Reverse Wireless Charging 244
Ringtone 178

S

S20 Ultra: Camera features and Tips
.... 263
Samsung Daily............................. 40, 41
Samsung Notes.............71, 142, 143, 144
Samsung Pass 213

Samsung Pay 145, 146, 147
Scene optimizer 78, 81
Schedule Message........................... 256
Screen brightness 186
screen lock 17, 172, 209, 210
Screen mode 187
Screen Reader.................................. 226
Screen recorder 91
Screen saver..................................... 190
Screen zoom 188
Screenshot 249
Search for apps................................. 94
Secure Folder.....................................215
Set up 10, 18, 20
Settings 153
shooting mode 75, 79, 80
Side key settings 17
Simple Pay.. 146
Size and zoom.................................. 228
Smart alert.. 184
Smart Select..................................... 57
Smart stay...192
SmartThings 102
Software update.............................. 203
Sound mode..............................112, 175
Status Bar 245
Status bar.. 36
Stopwatch 110
SUPER OPTIC ZOOM FEATURE: .. 274
System sound....................................179
System vibration.............................. 180

T

Take Photos 250
Tap and pay 162
Text display 230
Themes 46
Timeout settings 168
Toolbar 65
Tools 58, 122, 123
Touch sensitivity 190
Touch settings 232
Transfer Data 16
TRUE ZOOM FEATURE: 273
TTY mode 140
Turn on 15, 47, 70, 123, 148, 156, 164, 168, 186, 187, 191, 192, 212, 260

V

Videos 82
Visibility enhancements 226
voice input 67, 68, 69
Voicemail 138
Volume 177
VPN 172

W

Wake Up 252
Weather 110
Wi-Fi 154
Wi-Fi Direct 157

Z

ZOOM 269

Printed in the USA
CPSIA information can be obtained
at www.ICGtesting.com
LVHW021554221024
794538LV00007B/355